Modes of Writing

DESCRIPTIONS

Janet Goodwyn and Andrew Goodwyn

Series editor: Richard Andrews

CAMBRIDGE
UNIVERSITY PRESS

Published by the Press Syndicate of the University of Cambridge
The Pitt Building, Trumpington Street, Cambridge CB2 IRP
40 West 20th Street, New York, NY 10011-4211, USA
10 Stamford Road, Oakleigh, Victoria 3166, Australia

© Cambridge University Press 1992

First published 1992

Printed in Great Britain

A catalogue record for this book is available from the British Library

ISBN 0 521 39969 6 Paperback

Produced by Zoë Books Limited
15, Worthy Lane, Winchester,
Hampshire SO23 7AB

Designed by Sterling Associates
Artwork by Linda Combi
Picture Research by Valerie Randall

Cover design by Linda Combi

MODES OF WRITING

Modes of Writing is a series which aims to bring a wide range of writing to the attention of students aged fourteen and upwards. It consists of three anthologies: *Narratives*, *Arguments* and *Descriptions*.

Narratives is a collection of stories, anecdotes, tales, comic strips, myths, fables and letters, all of which depend on the linking of events and states of mind in a sequence. The sequence takes place in time, though the 'events' may not necessarily be told in chronological order. Indeed, one of the points of this collection is to show that playing with time rather than simply representing time in writing is what narrative enables us to do. Another of the intentions here is to make it clear that narrative can be used not only to tell one's own story (as in autobiography), or in fiction, but also to record scientific observations, to argue a case (as in fables) and as a way of thinking.

Arguments includes everything from letters by Groucho Marx to a letter from a parent to a headteacher about school uniform; from cartoons to travel writing; from poems to a Monty Python script. Here it is the putting over of a point of view that is the focus rather than the telling of a sequence of events. The interrelationship of ideas is of more interest than the relationship with time. People are using language to persuade others to adopt their point of view, and they are using language in a much more varied way than the conventional 'essay' suggests (or allows).

The third book in the series, **Descriptions**, covers the range of writing which attempts to stay close to things in the world. Sometimes it uses narrative (as in reports), and at other times it argues a point simply through describing what it sees. On further occasions - in commentary, in conveying its subject matter in the present tense - it depends on neither of these methods, but appears to have a life of its own. It moves easily backwards and forwards between the 'real world' and the worlds of fiction (though it also sees the real world as one of a number of possible worlds).

If there appears to be a degree of overlap between these three books, that is part of the plan. These are not watertight categories with their own rules, but ways of organising writing which are flexible and which can be combined. Part of the aim of the series is to encourage invention, risk-taking and cross-over between these modes of composition, in 'English' and in other subjects.

By building the series on the principle of broad modes of writing rather than by themes or authors, we also draw attention to the different types of language that are available to writers as they compose. This is a series *about* language as well as one which is promoting the use of language in lively, productive and entertaining ways.

Lastly, we have wanted to produce books that are arguments in themselves: books which present a certain vision of the possibilities in language, but which are also there to argue with. To this end, we have tried to demystify the process of compiling the anthologies. We have demonstrated the thinking that has led to a particular choice of text or to a particular sequencing of texts. We hope that you will use these books critically; enter into a dialogue with the texts and go beyond the suggestions we have made in the activities.

Richard Andrews

CONTENTS

INTRODUCTION

We are all observers. Whatever we are doing or saying, wherever we are going or have been, we are noticing the world around us and the world within us. Our experience is our own, unique, but what makes life interesting is our passion for describing and explaining it. Our descriptions can range from the familiar answer to 'What did you do at school today?' to our attempts to define the most extraordinary events in human history.

Descriptions are everywhere. We find them in every conceivable conversation and in every type of writing. Every picture and every photograph is a frozen description of a specific place and moment. The poet and the scientist are both concerned with exact descriptions through very precise use of language, yet how different their writing can be.

This collection shows how varied is the art of description. We have tried to provide as rich a range of examples as possible, from different times and places, in varying styles and on a kaleidoscope of subjects. We have included writing from different contexts: imaginative, scientific, poetic, informative, narrative, discursive and many others. One important point is that description is everywhere; sometimes you can say categorically 'that is a piece of description' but even then that piece may be a part of a larger text containing many forms of writing.

We hope you will enjoy this collection. No description, however plain and simple, need be dull; no description however detailed and elaborate need be confusing.

This is not a text-book nor a course-book. There is no simple formula which proves that 'this plus that' equals a good description. Fortunately good writing is more human and more interesting than a formula. This book is a collection which we hope is of value in itself. The activities are intended to help you make use of the pieces in the book; we hope they will stimulate your own ideas and your own descriptive powers.

Janet Goodwyn   Andrew Goodwyn

BEING

Self Portrait

Vincent Van Gogh

Mirror

I am silver and exact. I have no preconceptions.
Whatever I see I swallow immediately
Just as it is, unmisted by love or dislike.
I am not cruel, only truthful -
The eye of a little god, four-cornered.
Most of the time I meditate on the opposite wall.
It is pink, with speckles. I have looked at it so long
I think it is a part of my heart. But it flickers.
Faces and darkness separate us over and over.

Now I am a lake. A woman bends over me,
Searching my reaches for what she really is.
Then she turns to those liars, the candles or the moon.
I see her back, and reflect it faithfully.
She rewards me with tears and an agitation of hands.
I am important to her. She comes and goes.
Each morning it is her face that replaces the darkness.
In me she has drowned a young girl, and in me an old woman
Rises toward her day after day, like a terrible fish.

Sylvia Plath

I'm

I'm   leaves of autumn flickering
and   the soles of shoes trampling
I'm   rotten eggs
and   the falcon sitting on them
I'm   the crack of a branch weighted by snow
and   the snow piling up
I'm   the point of a nail
and   the head of a nail
I'm   the current of a river
and   a drowned body floating down it
I'm   red-hot tongs
and   the palm seizing them
I'm   the inside of a rock
and   the outside of a rock
I'm   a bucket with no bottom
and   the man drawing water with it

Takano Kikuo

A Near Miss

Stephen was driving a hired car along a deserted minor road, eastwards towards central Suffolk. The sunroof was open wide. He had tired of searching for tolerable music on the radio and was content with the rush of warm air and the novelty of driving for the first time in over a year. A postcard he had written to Julie was in his back pocket. She seemed to want to be left alone. He was uncertain whether to post it. The sun was high behind him, giving a visibility of luminous clarity. The road was flanked by concrete irrigation ditches and made wide curves through miles of conifer plantation set well back beyond a wide swathe of tree stumps and dried out bracken. He had slept well the night before, he remembered later. He was relaxed but reasonably alert. His speed was somewhere between seventy and seventy-five, which dropped only a little as he came up behind a large pink lorry.

In what followed, the rapidity of events was accommodated by the slowing of time. He was preparing to overtake when something happened - he did not quite see what - in the region of the lorry's wheels, a hiatus, a cloud of dust, and then something black and long snaked through a hundred feet towards him. It slapped the windscreen, clung there a moment and was whisked away before he had time to understand what it was. And then - or did this happen in the same moment? - the rear of the lorry made a complicated set of movements, a bouncing and swaying, and slewed in a wide spray of sparks, bright even in sunshine. Something curved and metallic flew off to one side. So far Stephen had had time to move his foot towards the brake, time to notice a padlock swinging on a loose flange, and 'Wash me please' scrawled in grime. There was a whinnying of scraped metal and new sparks, dense enough to form a white flame which seemed to propel the rear of the lorry into the air. He was applying first pressure to the brake as he saw the dusty, spinning wheels, the oily bulge of the differential, the camshaft, and now, at eye level, the base of the gear box. The upended lorry bounced on its nose once, perhaps twice, then lazily, tentatively, began to complete the somersault, bringing Stephen the inverted radiator grill, the downward flash of windscreen and a deep boom as the roof hit the road, rose again several feet, fell back, and surged along before him on a bed of flame. Then it swung its length round to block the road, fell on to its side and stopped abruptly as Stephen headed into it from a distance of less than a hundred feet and at a speed which he estimated, in a detached kind of way, to be forty-five miles an hour.

Now, in this slowing of time, there was a sense of a fresh beginning. He had entered a much later period in which all the terms and conditions had changed. So these were the new rules, and he experienced something like awe, as though he were walking alone into a great city on a newly discovered planet. There was space too for a little touch of regret, genuine nostalgia for the old days of spectacle, back then when a lorry used to caterpult so impressively before the impassive witness. Now was a more demanding time of effort and concentration. He was pointing the car towards a six-foot gap formed between a road sign and the front bumper of the motionless lorry. He had removed his foot from the brakes, reasoning - and it was as if he had just completed a monograph on the subject - that they were pulling the car to one side, interfering with his aim. Instead he was changing down through the gears and steering with both hands firmly, but not too tightly, on the wheel, ready to bring them up to cover his head if he missed. He beamed messages, or rather messages sprang from him, to Julie and Kate, nothing more distinct than pulses of alarm and love. There were others he should send to, he knew, but time was short, less than half a second, and fortunately they did not come to mind to confuse him. As he shifted to second and the small car gave out a protesting roar, it was clear that he must not think too hard, that he had to trust to a relaxed and dissociated thinking, that he must imagine himself into the gap. On the sound of this very word, which he must have spoken aloud, there was a brisk crunch of metal and glass and he was through and coming to a halt, with his door handle and wing mirror scattered across the road fifty feet behind.

Ian McEwan

my father is a retired magician

(for ifa, p.t., & bisa)

my father is a retired magician
which accounts for my irregular behavior
everythin comes outta magic hats
or bottles wit no bottoms & parakeets
are as easy to get as a couple a rabbits
or 3 fifty cent pieces / 1958

my daddy retired from magic & took
up another trade cuz this friend of mine
from the 3rd grade asked to be made white
on the spot

what cd any self-respectin colored american magician
do wit such a outlandish request / cept
put all them razzamatazz hocus pocus zippity-do-dah
thingamajigs away   cuz
colored chirren believin in magic
waz becomin politically dangerous for the race
& waznt nobody gonna be made white
on the spot   just
from a clap of my daddy's hands

& the reason i'm so peculiar's
cuz i been studyin up on my daddy's technique
& everythin i do is magic these days
& it's very colored
very now you see it / now you
don't mess wit me
                i come from a family of retired
sorcerers / active houngans & pennyante fortune tellers
wit 41 million spirits critturs & celestial bodies
on our side

      i'll listen to yr problems
      help wit yr career   yr lover   yr wanderin spouse
      make yr grandma's stay in heaven more gratifyin
      ease yr mother thru menopause & show yr son
      how to clean his room

YES YES YES   3 wishes is all you get
     scarlet ribbons for yr hair
         benwa balls via hong kong
             a miniature of machu picchu

all things are possible
but aint no colored magician in her right mind
gonna make you   white
    i mean
         this is blk magic
you lookin at
             & i'm fixin you up good / fixin you up
             good n colored
& you gonna be colored all yr life
& you gonna love it / bein colored / all yr life / colored & love it
love it / bein colored /

SPELL #7 FROM UPNORTH-OUTWEST GEECHEE JIBARA
QUIK MAGIC TRANCE MANUAL FOR TECHNOLOGICALLY
STRESSED THIRD WORLD PEOPLE

Ntozake Shange

Tokyo Pastoral

This is clearly one of those districts where it always seems to be
Sunday afternoon. Somebody in a house by the corner shop is
effortlessly practising Chopin on the piano. A dusty cat rolls in the
ruts of the unpaved streetlet, yawning in the sunshine. Somebody's
aged granny trots off to the supermarket for a litre or two of

honourable saki. Her iron-grey hair is scraped into so tight a knot in the nape no single hair could ever stray untidily out, and her decent, drab kimono is enveloped in the whitest of enormous aprons, trimmed with a sober frill of cotton lace, the kind of apron one associates with Victorian nursemaids.

She is bent to a full hoop because of all the babies she has carried on her back and she bows formally before she shows a socially acceptable quantity of her gold-rimmed teeth in a dignified smile. Frail, omnipotent granny who wields a rod of iron behind the paper walls.

This is a district peculiarly rich in grannies, cats and small children. We are a 60 yen train ride from the Marunouchi district, the great business section; and a 60 yen train ride in the other direction from Shinjuku, where there is the world's largest congregation of strip-shows, clip-joints and Turkish baths. We are a pretty bourgeois enclave of perpetual Sunday wedged between two mega-highways.

The sounds are: the brisk swish of broom on tatami matting, the raucous cawing of hooded crows in a nearby willow grove; clickety-clackety rattle of chattering housewives, a sound like briskly plied knitting needles, for Japanese is a language full of Ts and Ks; and, in the mornings, the crowing of a cock. The nights have a rustic tranquillity. We owe our tranquillity entirely to faulty town planning; these streets are far too narrow to admit cars. The smells are: cooking; sewage; fresh washing.

It is difficult to find a boring part of Tokyo but, by God, I have done it. It is a very respectable neighbourhood and has the prim charm and the inescapable accompanying ennui of respectability.

I can touch the walls of the houses on either side by reaching out my arms and the wall of the house at the back by stretching out my hand, but the fragile structures somehow contrive to be detached, even if there is only a clearance of inches between them, as though they were stating emphatically that privacy, even if it does not actually exist, is, at least, a potential. Most homes draw drab, grey skirts of breeze-block walls around themselves with the touch-me-not decorum of old maids, but even the tiniest of gardens boasts an exceedingly green tree or two and the windowsills bristle with potted plants.

Our neighbourhood is too respectable to be picturesque but, nevertheless, has considerable cosy charm, a higgledy-piggledy huddle of brown-grey shingled roofs and shining spring foliage. In the mornings, gaudy quilts, brilliantly patterned mattresses and cages of singing birds are hung out to air on the balconies. If the Japanese aesthetic ideal is a subfusc, harmonious austerity, the cultural norm is a homey, cheerful clutter. One must cultivate cosiness; cosiness makes overcrowding tolerable. Symmetrical lines of very clean washing blow in the wind. You could eat your dinner off the children. It is an area of white-collar workers; it is a good area.

The absolute domestic calm is disturbed by little more than the

occasional bicycle or a boy on a motorbike delivering a trayful of lacquer noodle bowls from the cafe on the corner for somebody's lunch or supper. In the morning, the men go off to work in business uniform (dark suits, white nylon shirts); in the afternoon, schoolchildren loll about eating ice-cream. High school girls wear navy-blue pleated skirts and sailor tops, very Edith Nesbitt, and high school boys wear high-collared blackjackets and peaked caps, inexpressibly Maxim Gorki.

At night, a very respectable drunk or two staggers, giggling, down the hill. A pragmatic race, the Japanese appear to have decided long ago that the only reason for drinking alcohol is to become intoxicated and therefore drink only when they wish to be drunk. They all are completely unabashed about it.

Although this is such a quiet district, the streets around the station contain everything a reasonable man might require. There is a blue movie theatre; a cinema that specialises in Italian and Japanese Westerns of hideous violence; a cinema that specialises in domestic consumption Japanese weepies; and yet another one currently showing *My Fair Lady*. There is a tintinabulation of chinking *pachinko* (pinball) parlours, several bakeries which sell improbably luxurious European pâtisserie, a gymnasium and an aphrodisiac shop or two.

If it lacks the excitement of most of the towns that, added up, amount to a massive and ill-plumbed concept called Greater Tokyo, that is because it is primarily a residential area, although one may easily find the cluster of hotels which offer hospitality by the hour. They are sited sedately up a side street by the station, off a turning by a festering rubbish tip outside a Chinese restaurant, and no neighbourhood, however respectable, is complete without them - for, in Japan, even the brothels are altogether respectable.

They are always scrupulously clean and cosy and the more expensive ones are very beautiful, with their windbells, stone lanterns and little rock gardens with streams, pools and water lilies. So elegantly homelike are they indeed, that the occasional erotic accessory - a red light bulb in the bedside light, a machine that emits five minutes of enthusiastic moans, grunts and pants at the insertion of a 100 yen coin - seems like a bad joke in a foreign language. Repression operates in every sphere but the sexual, even if privacy may only be purchased at extortionate rates.

There are few pleasant walks around here; the tree-shaded avenue beside the river offers delight only to coprophiles. But it is a joy to go out shopping. Since this is Japan, warped tomatoes and knobbly apples cost half the price of perfect fruit. It is the strawberry season; the man in the open fruit shop packs martial rows of berries the size of thumbs, each berry red as a guardsman, into a polythene box and wraps each box before he sells it in paper printed with the legend, 'Strawberry for health and beauty.'

Non-indigenous foods often taste as if they had been assembled from a blueprint by a man who had never seen the real thing. For example, cheese, butter and milk have such a degree of hygienic lack of tang they are wholly alienated from the natural cow. They taste absolutely, though not unpleasantly, synthetic and somehow indefinably obscene. Powdered cream (trade-named 'Creap') is less obtrusive in one's coffee. Most people, in fact, tend to use evaporated milk.

Tokyo ought not be a happy city - no pavements; noise; few public places to sit down; occasional malodorous belches from sewage vents even in the best areas; and yesterday I saw a rat in the supermarket. It dashed out from under the seaweed counter and went to earth in the butchery. "*Asoka,*" said the assistant, which means: "Well, well, I never did," in so far as the phrase could be said to mean anything. But, final triumph of ingenuity, Megapolis One somehow contrives to be an exceedingly pleasant place in which to live. It is as though Fellini had decided to remake *Alphaville.*

Up the road, there is a poodle-clipping parlour; a Pepsi-Cola bottling plant heavily patrolled by the fuzz; a noodle shop which boasts a colour TV; a mattress shop which also sells wicker neck-pillows of antique design; innumerable bookshops, each with a shelf or two of European books, souvenirs of those who have passed this way before - a tattered paperback of *The Rosy Crucifixion,* a treatise on budgerigar keeping, Marx and Engels on England; a dispenser from which one may purchase condoms attractively packed in purple and gold paper, trademarked 'Young Jelly'; and a swimming pool.

I am the first coloured family in this street. I moved in on the Emperor's birthday, so the children were all home from school. They were playing 'catch' around the back of the house and a little boy came to hide in the embrasure of the window. He glanced round and caught sight of me. He did not register shock but he vanished immediately. Then there was a silence and, shortly afterwards, a soft thunder of tiny footsteps. They groped round the windows, invisible, peering, and a rustle rose up, like the dry murmur of dead leaves in the wind, the rustle of immeasurable small voices murmuring the word: "*Gaijin, gaijin, gaijin*" (foreigner), in pure, repressed surprise. We spy strangers. *Asoka.*

Angela Carter

Theme for English B

The instructor said,

> *Go home and write*
> *a page tonight.*
> *And let that page come out of you -*
> *Then, it will be true.*

I wonder if it's that simple?

I am twenty-two, colored, born in Winston-Salem.
I went to school there, then Durham, then here
to this college on the hill above Harlem.
I am the only colored student in my class.
The steps from the hill lead down into Harlem,
through a park, then I cross St Nicholas,
Eighth Avenue, Seventh, and I come to the Y,
the Harlem Branch Y, where I take the elevator
up to my room, sit down, and write this page:

It is not easy to know what is true for you or me
at twenty-two, my age. But I guess I'm what
I feel and see and hear, Harlem, I hear you:
hear you, hear me - we two - you, me, talk on this page.
(I hear New York, too.) Me - who?
Well, I like to eat, sleep, drink, and be in love.
I like to work, read, learn, and understand life.
I like a pipe for a Christmas present,
or records - Bessie, bop, or Bach.
I guess being colored doesn't make me *not* like
the same things other folks like who are other races.
So will my page be colored that I write?
Being me, it will not be white.
But it will be
a part of you, instructor.
You are white -
yet a part of me, as I am part of you.
That's American.
Sometimes perhaps you don't want to be a part of me.
Nor do I often want to be a part of you.
But we are, that's true!
As I learn from you,
I guess you learn from me -
although you're older - and white -
and somewhat more free.

This is my page for English B.

Langston Hughes

The Autobiography of Malcolm X

When my mother was pregnant with me, she told me later, a party of
hooded Ku Klux Klan riders galloped up to our home in Omaha,
Nebraska, one night. Surrounding the house, brandishing their
shotguns and rifles, they shouted for my father to come out. My

mother went to the front door and opened it. Standing where they could see her pregnant condition, she told them that she was alone with her three small children, and that my father was away, preaching, in Milwaukee. The Klansmen shouted threats and warnings at her that we had better get out of town because 'the good Christian white people' were not going to stand for my father's 'spreading trouble' among the 'good' Negroes of Omaha with the 'back to Africa' preachings of Marcus Garvey.

My father, the Reverend Earl Little, was a Baptist minister, a dedicated organizer for Marcus Aurelius Garvey's U.N.I.A. (Universal Negro Improvement Association). With the help of such disciples as my father, Garvey, from his headquarters in New York City's Harlem, was raising the banner of black-race purity and exhorting the Negro masses to return to their ancestral African homeland - a cause which had made Garvey the most controversial black man on earth.

Still shouting threats, the Klansmen finally spurred their horses and galloped around the house, shattering every window pane with their gun butts. Then they rode off into the night, their torches flaring, as suddenly as they had come.

My father was enraged when he returned. He decided to wait until I was born - which would be soon - and then the family would move. I am not sure why he made this decision, for he was not a frightened Negro, as most then were, and many still are today. My father was a big, six-foot-four, very black man. He had only one eye. How he had lost the other one I have never known. He was from Reynolds, Georgia, where he had left school after the third or maybe fourth grade. He believed, as did Marcus Garvey, that freedom, independence and self-respect could never be achieved by the Negro in America, and that therefore the Negro should leave America to the white man and return to his African land of origin. Among the reasons my father had decided to risk and dedicate his life to help disseminate this philosophy among his people was that he had seen four of his six brothers die by violence, three of them killed by white men, including one by lynching. What my father could not know then was that of the remaining three, including himself, only one, my Uncle Jim, would die in bed, of natural causes. Northern white police were later to shoot my Uncle Oscar. And my father was finally himself to die by the white man's hands.

It has always been my belief that I, too, will die by violence. I have done all that I can to be prepared.

I was my father's seventh child. He had three children by a previous marriage - Ella, Earl, and Mary, who lived in Boston. He had met and married my mother in Philadelphia, where their first child, my oldest full brother, Wilfred, was born. They moved from Philadelphia to Omaha, where Hilda and then Philbert were born.

I was next in line. My mother was twenty-eight when I was born on May 19, 1925, in an Omaha hospital. Then we moved to

Milwaukee, where Reginald was born. From infancy, he had some kind of hernia condition which was to handicap him physically for the rest of his life.

Louise Little, my mother, who was born in Grenada, in the British West Indies, looked like a white woman. Her father *was* white. She had straight black hair, and her accent did not sound like a Negro's. Of this white father of hers, I know nothing except her shame about it. I remember hearing her say she was glad that she had never seen him. It was, of course, because of him that I got my reddish-brown 'mariny' color of skin, and my hair of the same color. I was the lightest child in our family. (Out in the world later on, in Boston and New York, I was among the millions of Negroes who were insane enough to feel that it was some kind of status symbol to be light-complexioned - that one was actually fortunate to be born thus. But, still later, I learned to hate every drop of that white rapist's blood that is in me.)

Our family stayed only briefly in Milwaukee, for my father wanted to find a place where he could raise our own food and perhaps build a business. The teaching of Marcus Garvey stressed becoming independent of the white man. We went next, for some reason, to Lansing, Michigan. My father bought a house and soon, as had been his pattern, he was doing free-lance Christian preaching in local Negro Baptist churches, and during the week he was roaming about spreading word of Marcus Garvey.

He had begun to lay away savings for the store he had always wanted to own when, as always, some stupid local Uncle Tom Negroes began to funnel stories about his revolutionary beliefs to the local white people. This time, the get-out-of-town threats came from a local hate society called The Black Legion. They wore black robes instead of white. Soon, nearly everywhere my father went, Black Legionnaires were reviling him as an 'uppity nigger' for wanting to own a store, for living outside the Lansing Negro district, for spreading unrest and dissension among 'the good niggers.'

As in Omaha, my mother was pregnant again, this time with my youngest sister. Shortly after Yvonne was born came the nightmare night in 1929, my earliest vivid memory. I remember being suddenly snatched awake into a frightening confusion of pistol shots and shouting and smoke and flames. My father had shouted and shot at the two white men who had set the fire and were running away. Our home was burning down around us. We were lunging and bumping and tumbling all over each other trying to escape. My mother, with the baby in her arms, just made it into the yard before the house crashed in, showering sparks. I remember we were outside in the night in our underwear, crying and yelling our heads off. The white police and firemen came and stood around watching as the house burned down to the ground.

My father prevailed on some friends to clothe and house us temporarily; then he moved us into another house on the outskirts of

East Lansing. In those days Negroes weren't allowed after dark in East Lansing proper. There's where Michigan State University is located: I related all of this to an audience of students when I spoke there in January, 1963 (and had the first reunion in a long while with my younger brother, Robert, who was there doing postgraduate studies in psychology). I told them how East Lansing harassed us so much that we had to move again, this time two miles out of town, into the country. This was where my father built for us with his own hands a four-room house. This is where I really begin to remember things - this home where I started to grow up.

After the fire, I remember that my father was called in and questioned about a permit for the pistol with which he had shot at the white men who set the fire. I remember that the police were always dropping by our house, shoving things around, 'just checking' or 'looking for a gun'. The pistol they were looking for - which they never found, and for which they wouldn't issue a permit - was sewed up inside a pillow. My father's .22 rifle and his shotgun, though, were right out in the open; everyone had them for hunting birds and rabbits and other game.

Malcolm X

SEEING

Resemblances

Always I look for some reminding feature,
Compel a likeness where there is not one,
As in a gallery I trace the stature
Of that one's boldness or of this one's grace.
Yet likenesses so searched for will yield none;
One feature, yes, but never the whole face.

So every face falls back into its parts
And once-known glances leave the candid look
Of total strangeness. Where the likeness starts
We fix attention, set aside the rest,
As those who scan for notes a thick-packed book,
Recalling only what has pleased them best.

And doing this, so often I have missed
Some recognition never known before,
Some knowledge which I never could have guessed.
And how if all the others whom I pass
Should like myself be always searching for
The special features only one face has?

Always the dear enchanted moment stays.
We cannot unlearn all whom we have loved;
Who can tear off like calendars the days
Or wipe out features fixed within the mind?
Only there should be some way to be moved
Beyond the likeness to the look behind.

Elizabeth Jennings

My Daughter Smokes

My daughter smokes. While she is doing her homework, her feet on
the bench in front of her and her calculator clicking out answers to
her algebra problems, I am looking at the half-empty package of
Camels tossed carelessly close at hand. Camels. I pick them up, take
them into the kitchen, where the light is better, and study them -
they're filtered, for which I am grateful. My heart feels terrible. I
want to weep. In fact, I do weep a little, standing there by the stove

holding one of the instruments, so white, so precisely rolled, that could cause my daughter's death. When she smoked Marlboros and Players I hardened myself against feeling so bad; nobody I knew ever smoked these brands.

She doesn't know this, but it was Camels that my father, her grandfather, smoked. But before he smoked 'ready-mades' - when he was very young and very poor, with eyes like lanterns - he smoked Prince Albert tobacco in cigarettes he rolled himself. I remember the bright-red tobacco tin, with a picture of Queen Victoria's consort, Prince Albert, dressed in a black frock coat and carrying a cane.

The tobacco was dark brown, pungent, slightly bitter. I tasted it more than once as a child, and the discarded tins could be used for a number of things: to keep buttons and shoelaces in, to store seeds, and best of all, to hold worms for the rare times my father took us fishing.

By the late forties and early fifties no one rolled his own anymore (and few women smoked) in my hometown, Eatonton, Georgia. The tobacco industry, coupled with Hollywood movies in which both hero and heroine smoked like chimneys, won over completely people like my father, who were hopelessly addicted to cigarettes. He never looked as dapper as Prince Albert, though; he continued to look like a poor, overweight, overworked colored man with too large a family; black, with a very white cigarette stuck in his mouth.

I do not remember when he started to cough. Perhaps it was unnoticeable at first. A little hacking in the morning as he lit his first cigarette upon getting out of bed. By the time I was my daughter's age, his breath was a wheeze, embarrassing to hear; he could not climb stairs without resting every third or fourth step. It was not unusual for him to cough for an hour.

It is hard to believe there was a time when people did not understand that cigarette smoking is an addiction. I wondered aloud once to my sister - who is perennially trying to quit - whether our father realized this. I wondered how she, a smoker since high school, viewed her own habit.

It was our father who gave her her first cigarette, one day when she had taken water to him in the fields.

"I always wondered why he did that," she said, puzzled, and with some bitterness.

"What did he say?" I asked.

"That he didn't want me to go to anyone else for them," she said, "which never really crossed my mind."

So he was aware it was addictive, I thought, though as annoyed as she that he assumed she would be interested.

I began smoking in eleventh grade, also the year I drank numerous bottles of terrible sweet, very cheap wine. My friends and I, all boys for this venture, bought our supplies from a man who ran a segregated bar and liquor store on the outskirts of town. Over the entrance there was a large sign that said COLORED. We were not permitted to drink there, only to buy. I smoked Kools, because my sister did. By then I thought her toxic darkened lips and gums glamorous. However, my body simply would not tolerate smoke. After six months I had a chronic sore throat. I gave up smoking, gladly. Because it was a ritual with my buddies - Murl, Leon, and 'Dog' Farley - I continued to drink wine.

My father died from 'the poor man's friend,' pneumonia, one hard winter when his bronchitis and emphysema had left him low. I doubt he had much lung left at all, after coughing for so many years. He had so little breath that, during his last years, he was always leaning on something. I remember once, at a family reunion, when my daughter was two, that my father picked her up for a minute - long enough for me to photograph them - but the effort was obvious. Near the very end of his life, and largely because he had no more lungs, he quit smoking. He gained a couple of pounds, but by then he was so emaciated no one noticed.

When I travel to Third World countries I see many people like my father and daughter. There are large billboards directed at them both: the tough, 'take-charge' or dapper older man, the glamorous, 'worldly' young woman, both puffing away. In these poor countries, as in American ghettos and on reservations, money that should be spent for food goes instead to the tobacco companies; over time, people starve themselves of both food and air, effectively weakening and addicting their children, eventually eradicating themselves. I read in the newspaper and in my gardening magazine that cigarette butts are so toxic that if a baby swallows one, it is likely to die, and that the boiled water from a bunch of them makes an effective insecticide.

My daughter would like to quit, she says. We both know the statistics are against her; most people who try to quit smoking do not succeed.*

There is a deep hurt that I feel as a mother. Some days it is a feeling of futility. I remember how carefully I ate when I was pregnant, how patiently I taught my daughter how to cross a street safely. For what, I sometimes wonder; so that she can wheeze through most of her life feeling half her strength, and then die of self-poisoning, as her grandfather did?

But, finally, one must feel empathy for the tobacco plant itself. For thousands of years, it has been venerated by Native Americans as a sacred medicine. They have used it extensively - its juice, its leaves, its roots, its (holy) smoke - to heal wounds and cure diseases, and in ceremonies of prayer and peace. And though the plant as most of us

* Three months after reading this essay my daughter stopped smoking.

know it has been poisoned by chemicals and denatured by intensive mono-cropping and is therefore hardly the plant it was, still, to some modern Indians it remains a plant of positive power. I learned this when my Native American friends, Bill Wahpepah and his family, visited with me for a few days and the first thing he did was sow a few tobacco seeds in my garden.

Perhaps we can liberate tobacco from those who have captured and abused it, enslaving the plant on large plantations, keeping it from freedom and its kin, and forcing it to enslave the world. Its true nature suppressed, no wonder it has become deadly. Maybe by sowing a few seeds of tobacco in our gardens and treating the plant with the reverence it deserves, we can redeem tobacco's soul and restore its self-respect.

Besides, how grim, if one is a smoker, to realize one is smoking a slave.

There is a slogan from a battered women's shelter that I especially like: 'Peace on earth begins at home.' I believe everything does. I think of a slogan for people trying to stop smoking: 'Every home a smoke-free zone.' Smoking is a form of self-battering that also batters those who must sit by, occasionally cajole or complain, and helplessly watch. I realize now that as a child I sat by, through the years, and literally watched my father kill himself: surely one such victory in my family, for the rich white men who own the tobacco companies, is enough.

Alice Walker

Sir Thomas More

SIR THOMAS MORE, Lord Chancellour: his Countrey-howse was at Chelsey, in Middlesex, where Sir John Danvers built his howse. Where the gate is now, adorned with two noble Pyramids, there stood anciently a Gate-house; which was flatt on the top, leaded, from whence there is a most pleasant prospect of the Thames and the fields beyond. On this place the Lord Chancellour More was wont to recreate himselfe and contemplate. It happened one time that a Tom of Bedlam came up to him, and had a Mind to have throwne him from the battlements, saying Leap, Tom, leap. The Chancellour was in his gowne, and besides ancient and not able to struggle with such a strong fellowe. My Lord had a little dog. Sayd he, Let us first throwe the dog downe, and see what sporte that will be. So the dog was throwne over. This is very fine sport, sayd my Lord, Let us fetch him up, and try once more. While the mad man was goeing downe, my Lord fastned the dore, and called for help, but ever after kept the dore shutt.

(Till the breaking-out of the Civil-warre, Tom o Bedlam's did travell about the Countrey: they had been poore distracted men that had been putt into Bedlam, where recovering to some sobernesse they were truncated to goe a begging, e.g. they had on their left arme an Armilla or Tinne printed in some workes: about 4 inches long: they could not gett it off. They wore about their necks a great Horne of an Oxe, in a string or Bawdrie, which, when they came to an house for Almes, they did sound; and they did putt the drinke given them into this Horne, whereto they did putt a stopple. Since the Warres I doe not remember to have seen anyone of them.)

In his *Utopia* his lawe is that the young people are to see each other stark-naked before marriage. Sir William Roper, of Eltham, in Kent, came one morning, pretty early, to my Lord, with a proposall to marry one of his daughters. My Lord's daughters were then both together abed in a truckle-bed in their father's chamber asleep. He carries Sir William into the chamber and takes the Sheete by the corner and suddenly whippes it off. They lay on their Backs, and their smocks up as high as their arme-pitts. This awakened them, and immediately they turned on their bellies. Quoth Roper, I have seen both sides, and so gave a patt on the buttock, he made choice of, sayeing, Thou art mine. Here was all the trouble of the wooeing. This account I had from my honoured friend old Mris Tyndale, whose grandfather, Sir William Stafford, was an intimate friend of this Sir W. Roper, who told him the story.

His discourse was extraordinary facetious [*amusing*]. Riding one night, upon the suddaine he crossed himself *majori cruce* [*with the great sign of the cross*] crying out Jesu Maria! doe not you see that prodigious Dragon in the skye? They all lookt up, and one did not see it, and nor the tother did not see it. At length one had spyed it, and at last all had spied. Whereas there was no such phantome, only he imposed on their phantasies.

After he was beheaded, his trunke was interred in Chelsey church, neer the middle of the South wall, where was some slight Monument erected. His head was upon London bridge. There goes this story in the family, viz. that one day as one of his daughters was passing under the Bridge, looking on her father's head, sayd she, That head haz layn many a time in my Lapp; would to God it would fall into my Lap as I passe under. She had her wish, and it did fall into her Lappe, and is now preserved in a vault in the Cathedral Church at Canterbury.

The Descendant of Sir Thomas, is Mr More of Chilston, in Herefordshire, where, among a great many things of value plundered by the Soldiers, was his Chap [*jawbone*], which they kept for a Relique. Methinks 'tis strange that all this time he is not Canonised, for he merited highly of the Church.

John Aubrey

The Butcher

'And even St George - if Gibbon is correct -
wore a top hat once; he was an army contractor
and supplied indifferent bacon'
(E. M. Forster, Abinger Harvest)

Surrounded by sausages, the butcher stands
smoking a pencil like Isambard Kingdom Brunel . . .

He duels with himself and woos his women customers,
offering thin coiled coral necklaces of mince,

heart lamé-ed from the fridge, a leg of pork
like a nasty bouquet, pound notes printed with blood.

He knows all about nudity - the slap and trickle
of blood, chickens stripped to their aertex vests.

He rips the gauze from dead balletic pigs,
and makes the bacon slicer swish its legs.

How the customers laugh! His striped apron
gets as dirty as the mattress in a brothel . . .

At 10, he drinks his tea with the spoon held back,
and the *Great Eastern* goes straight to the bottom.

Craig Raine

The Lavatory Attendant

'I counted two and seventy stenches
All well defined and several stinks!'
(Coleridge)

Slumped on a chair, his body is an S
That wants to be a minus sign.

His face is overripe Wensleydale
Going blue at the edges.

In overalls of sacerdotal white
He guards a row of fonts

With lids like eye-patches. Snapped shut
They are castanets. All day he hears
Short-lived Niagaras, the clank
And gurgle of canescent cisterns.

When evening comes he sluices a thin tide
Across sand-coloured lino,

Turns Medusa on her head
And wipes the floor with her.

Wendy Cope

OBSERVING

Anne Frank with a Telephone

In the heart of London one family stays together in their one large room, overlooking the street. They do not go outside after seven o'clock at night, neither do they go downstairs after dark. Only the dog, a worrying beast called Soldier, is downstairs, in the front room which was to be the father's tailor's shop and is now barricaded, on the urging of the police, who say they can do nothing.

The mother sits beside the window in the large room. She seldom moves from this watching position. Her bed has been moved there, beside the window; and when she talks her eyes remain fixed on the street below. Beside her is a plastic box filled with a variety of medicines, most of them anti-depressants and sleeping tablets and others for the relief of asthma. As each siege begins or appears imminent, she calls out names, names which are familiar to all the family. They are the names of their tormentors, led and inspired by fascist and racist groups, some of them dating back to January 1983 when the family moved into the house.

"They go in circles," said the eldest daughter, Nasreen, who is sixteen. "They go round and round. Or maybe they just sit, and do nothing at all. Or maybe they just hit the door or just throw rocks ... ."

"And shit," said her father, trying to smile.

"And shit," said Nasreen.

I met this family in the winter of 1983 when the attacks were most intense, and since then I have kept in regular contact with Nasreen. She is the voice of her parents, who came to Britain from Pakistan twenty-one years ago, and of her teenage sister and brother, who, like her, were born and brought up in the East End of London. The conversations I have with Nasreen on the telephone run to a pattern. "Nasreen 'ere," she says in her cockney accent. "They're at the door now. Hear 'em? I've called the police and they're comin', they say ... that's all. Bye."

She may ring back to say they are all right. She may ask me to ring Newham Council the next day and occasionally the police that night, but more often than not she asks nothing; she is merely making contact with the world outside her barricades. She always reminds me of Anne Frank, the Jewish girl who hid in the attic of her home in Amsterdam during the Nazi occupation and kept a diary of her life. She is Anne Frank with a telephone.

Nasreen's diaries are material for future historians who wish to look beneath the 1980s surface of British society, of which her father's family, before they came from the Punjab, used to speak as 'a place of free dreams'. The first entry in Nasreen's diary was during the week they moved in, having invested all their savings and taken out a mortgage; this was to be a new life.

On the night of January 25, 1983 a gang of forty attacked. They threw stones, smashing the shop windows and missing the family by inches. They daubed swastikas and gave Nazi salutes and chanted, "Fucking Pakis out!" They did this for six straight hours. Nasreen wrote this in her diary:

> When the trouble started, we phone the police, but they never came. Then again we phone the police, but they never came. Then my father went to the police station to get the police . . . we had a witness. The police said they didn't need a witness.

The entries in the diary for the days and weeks that followed, often written by candlelight or in freezing darkness as the family huddled in an upstairs room, were repetitive and to the point: 'Trouble. Got no sleep. Had no telephone . . . three or four of them throw stones at our window.'

Today, the family is still prevented by menace and violence from opening the shop they own. For a time her father worked in the most secure room, in the back. Then a stone narrowly missed his head and he became ill. He seldom comes downstairs at all now, and in the winter and autumn they are usually all inside by five in the afternoon. Nasreen describes her life as 'sort of like living under a table'.

The casual brutality this family has experienced is typical of that endured by numerous families of Asian origin and has now reached a level reminiscent of the racist attacks on East End Jews in the 1930s. The Home Office has estimated that Asians are fifty times more likely to be attacked than white people, although few of these attacks are reported in newspapers or on television, let alone to the police.

Newham police told me they gave the family 'special attention' but that it was impossible to mount 'a twenty-four-hour guard'. Had they, I asked, prosecuted anybody in connection with the attacks? A senior officer said that it was difficult to prosecute because "They are mostly juveniles." This was an unconvincing explanation as more juveniles are being prosecuted now than ever before, with racist bullies the exceptions.

Alongside Nasreen's diary is a growing file of correspondence with the police, the Home Office, the local authority, the local MP and the prime minister. She has tried to make the nominal system of accountable government and law work to protect her family. She began by writing a sheaf of letters to Arthur Lewis, then the Labour MP for Newham North-West. She was fourteen then. She wrote:

Dear Mr Lewis,
We are an Asian family under attack by the National Front and similar group. My mother has not slept for the last two months and has had to go to hospital for several days. We cannot furnish or decorate our home because we are too busy looking out through the window day and night, ensuring nobody attacks our house. The police seem to come only when you either phone

them or write to them, or when they feel they are being watched by people such as you. Since the attacks began they failed to arrest one person, even though they know who they are. You say in your letter that our problem is housing. We have a house, Mr Lewis, and we want to stay in the house. I ask you for your help [and the] local Labour Party members to come and defend us. People have died this year, by attack, and the police never protected them.

Yours sincerely,
Nasreen

On March 29, 1983 Arthur Lewis told the House of Commons that the family had been 'smashed about by skinheads'. Mrs Thatcher replied that the then Home Secretary, William Whitelaw, was 'taking up the matter'. Mr Whitelaw is now in the House of Lords. The matter was never taken up. In the meantime Nasreen had written to Newham Council housing department saying, 'We cannot go on living under attack all the time.' Her mother, on one rare expedition to the shops, was surrounded by a gang and spat at.

The Council offered the family a house, but they could not afford both to rent it and pay their mortgage, and while their present house was barricaded and smothered with graffiti, they could not sell it. They were trapped. Two 'average' days in Nasreen's diary read:

9.10 p.m. There was a knock at the door. [Almost every night there is a knocking or the thud of a boot or the crash of a bottle.] I got out of bed and looked out the window. A driver shouted at us . . .
10 p.m. There were two boys sitting in the car park throwing stones at us . . . no sleep again.

In May 1983 Nasreen wrote to Mrs Thatcher:

Dear Margaret,
I understand that you were able to raise these matters when he deputised for you at Question Time . . . I am sorry to tell you that you don't understand our matter, Mrs Thatcher. You don't care if we get beaten up, do you?

My mother has asthma and she has to stay to 11 a.m. watching through the window because me and my brother and sister has to go to school. I can't stay home to look after my mother because I got exams to worry about. My father has blood pressure and if he loses his temper, what are we going to do? He is the only man to feed us. We have no money to repair our house since the kids in the street have damaged it. We are asking for your help, not your money, Mrs Thatcher.

Yours sincerely,
Nasreen

An extraordinary reply came, not from Mrs Thatcher but from a Mr C D Inge at the Home Office. Mr Inge urged the family to keep reporting every attack to the police 'even if the police are unable to take effective action'. In his final paragraph Mr Inge said:

I am sorry that I am not able to give you a more helpful reply, but let me take this opportunity to assure you that the Government does care about the incidence of racial attacks and is committed to a multi-racial society in which all can go without fear of racial violence or abuse.

This 'commitment' has yet to take effect. It is difficult to find an Asian family in East London who has not been attacked in one form or another. Nasreen's family have weathered their siege better than most. Not far from them lives an eleven-year-old Asian boy who wrote this essay at school:

The day we moved into the new house, we got up at six o'clock. We came to the estate, to wait for the electricity man. The neighbours came out and shouted, "Get those people out of here." The big boys shouted, "Send them out. Send them out. Send them out." These boys says, "Look, there's bugs in their bed and in the chairs."

The essay ends abruptly because its small author had to retreat inside his new home when a mob arrived. The mob consisted of adults leading teenagers and children and it blockaded the family's flat, taped up the door and let loose a German shepherd dog. The police were called and arrived after a long delay. They demanded to see the father's rent book to see if he was 'legal' - that is, legally entitled to be in Britain - which he was. Then they left; nobody was arrested. Most families under siege are too frightened to call the police for fear of being prosecuted themselves.

In 1982 the London region of the Fire Brigades Union asked its eleven divisions for details of the fire attacks on ethnic minorities. Walthamstow fire station listed thirteen cases, the most common being petrol poured through the letter box followed by a lighted paper. One of these incidents had appeared in the local press; none had featured in the national papers or on television. They happen in a world little known to most journalists and to those who live in places of suburban privacy. In a society kept divided and mutually antagonistic, the Asians serve a dual purpose. Part of the Asian population forms a new working class with many of the old illusions and expectations intact and so remains politically pliant; others fulfil their old imperial role as a shopkeeper class, allegedly Mrs Thatcher's favourite people. In Handsworth in 1985 this group felt particularly betrayed when their property was not protected. In both cases they serve as scapegoats for the frustrations of working-class people - white and black - whose expectations have long been undermined.

On the night I last visited Nasreen's family not much happened. The usual tormentors were there. Soldier, the dog chained in a room meant to be a tailor's shop, barked on cue. Nasreen ventured half-way down the stairs, but would go no farther. A stone smashed against their van, and there were human yowls outside their door. Later, when I had returned home and she phoned me as usual, not much more had happened. They got to sleep at one o'clock, when at last there was nobody down there.

John Pilger

Two Ways of Seeing a River

Now when I had mastered the language of this water and had come to know every trifling feature that bordered the great river as familiarly as I knew the letters of the alphabet, I had made a valuable acquisition. But I had lost something, too. I had lost something which could never be restored to me while I lived. All the grace, the beauty, the poetry, had gone out of the majestic river! I still kept in mind a certain wonderful sunset which I witnessed when steamboating was new to me. A broad expanse of the river was turned to blood; in the middle distance the red hue brightened into gold, through which a solitary log came floating, black and conspicuous; in one place a long, slanting mark lay sparkling upon the water; in another the surface was broken by boiling, tumbling rings, that were as many-tinted as an opal; where the ruddy flush was faintest, was a smooth spot that was covered with graceful circles and radiating lines, ever so delicately traced; the shore on our left was densely wooded and the somber shadow that fell from this forest was broken in one place by a long, ruffled trail that shone like silver; and high above the forest wall a clean-stemmed dead tree waved a single leafy bough that glowed like a flame in the unobstructed splendor that was flowing from the sun. There were graceful curves, reflected images, woody heights, soft distances, and over the whole scene, far and near, the dissolving lights drifted steadily, enriching it every passing moment with new marvels of coloring.

I stood like one bewitched. I drank it in, in a speechless rapture. The world was new to me and I had never seen anything like this at home. But as I have said, a day came when I began to cease from noting the glories and the charms which the moon and the sun and the twilight wrought upon the river's face; another day came when I ceased altogether to note them. Then, if that sunset scene had been repeated, I should have looked upon it without rapture, and should have commented upon it inwardly after this fashion: "This sun means that we are going to have wind to-morrow; that floating log means that the river is rising, small thanks to it; that slanting mark on the water refers to a bluff reef which is going to kill somebody's steamboat one of these nights, if it keeps on stretching out like that; those tumbling 'boils' show a dissolving bar and a changing channel there; the lines and circles in the slick water over yonder are a warning that that troublesome place is shoaling up dangerously; that silver streak in the shadow of the forest is the 'break' from a new snag and he has located himself in the very best place he could have found to fish for steamboats; that tall dead tree, with a single living branch, is not going to last long, and then how is a body ever going to get through this blind place at night without the friendly old landmark?"

No, the romance and beauty were all gone from the river. All the value any feature of it had for me now was the amount of usefulness it could furnish toward compassing the safe piloting of a steamboat. Since those days, I have pitied doctors from my heart. What does the lovely flush in a beauty's cheek mean to a doctor but a 'break' that ripples above some deadly disease? Are not all her visible charms sown thick with what are to him the signs and symbols of hidden decay? Does he ever see her beauty at all, or doesn't he simply view her professionally and comment upon her unwholesome condition all to himself? And doesn't he sometimes wonder whether he has gained most or lost most by learning his trade?

Mark Twain

Song of the Light-Bulb

A man once bought a light-bulb
and went home alone on the dark evening road
The young woman who sold him the light-bulb
was the shopkeeper's wife
and the man who bought the light-bulb
had once been secretly in love with her
He stood for a moment under the eaves
then left the spill of light from the window
and putting his feet one after the other
into the circles of light beneath the street-lamps
he went back alone
on the dark evening road

Kamimura Hajime

The Fridge

What a sturdy square block of a thing you are!
Such a fine, white, self-satisfied creature!

Sometimes you stand dumb as a boulder
or drop off into a cold sleep, or
sometimes your metal belly rumbles, but there's
no point in working out your meaning.

Of all machines the fridge must be the
most good-natured; hog-fat and
roomy as a snow-drift, it
must be said to hold the purest heart.

Firmly under human domination
even the cold that creeps out from it
is only a small cold blast, too small
to threaten any freeze-up of our future.

If ever robots rise in revolution,
if ever they attack the human race,
at least you refrigerators won't be
amongst the ones to break the peace.

For you are the house-dog of machinery
a faithful and contented animal;
so give your door a docile wag for Man,
your living friend, and show him how you smile.

Boris Slutsky
(Translated by Elaine Feinstein)

Downpipes

Evening rain
Through the downpipes
Damp walls
Green mould and moss.
Ah, those pipes -
With their round mouths,
They gossip to strangers
Their houses' secrets.

Downpipes
Your secrets give me no pleasure,
Rusty pipes
Stop telling tales -
I don't know you
I don't want your secrets
Knowing secrets
It's hard to dream dreams, or to love.

Yes, I believe
That behind this door
Or that window
There's injustice, and loss, and deceit,
I believe you!
But somehow I don't believe
And smile
At these stone-built houses.

I believe in hope
Even if it seems hopeless
I believe, even,
In a vain, quite impossible dream -
I see the town
I see the beautiful town
In white mist
In dark evening rain.

Poor downpipes
You're old -
All your mould
Is just the first bloom on your lips.
You're still old:
But we have grown young
Although we have known
The oldest pain.

Evening rain
Through the downpipes.
Damp walls
Green mould and moss.
Ah, those pipes -
Making round mouths
They gossip to strangers
Their houses' secrets.

Novella Matveyeva
(Translated by J. R. Rowland)

A Postcard from France

NICE, FRANCE
JANUARY 7, 1956

Dear Mother,

Yesterday was about the most lovely in my life. Started out on motor scooter along famous wide 'promenade des anglais' of Nice, with its out-door cafés, splendid baroque facades, rows of palms, strolling musicians - and headed inland to Vence, where I planned to see the beautiful recent Matisse Cathedral of my art magazine, which I've loved via pictures for years.

How can I describe the beauty of the country? Everything is so small, close, exquisite and fertile. Terraced gardens on steep slopes of rich, red earth, orange and lemon trees, olive orchards, tiny pink and peach houses. To Vence - small, on a sun-warmed hill, uncommercial, slow, peaceful. Walked to Matisse cathedral - small, pure, clean-cut. White with a blue tile roof sparkling in the sun. But shut! Only open to public two days a week. A kindly talkative peasant told me stories of how rich people came daily in large cars from Italy, Germany, Sweden, etc., and were not admitted, even for large sums of money. I was desolate and wandered to the back of the walled nunnery, where I could see a corner of the Chapel and sketched it, feeling like Alice outside the garden, watching the white doves and orange trees. Then I went back to the front and stared with my face through the barred gate. I began to cry. I knew it was so lovely inside, pure white with the sun through blue, yellow, and green stained windows.

Then I heard a voice, "Ne pleurez plus, entrez," and the Mother Superior let me in, after denying all the wealthy people in cars.

I just knelt in the heart of sun and colors of sky, sea, and sun, in the pure white heart of the Chapel. " Vous êtes si gentille," I stammered. The nun smiled. "C'est la miséricorde de Dieu." It was.

Love,
Sylvia

Sylvia Plath

The Driver Ants

The Ecitons, or foraging ants, are very numerous throughout Central America. Whilst the leaf-cutting ants are entirely vegetable feeders, the foraging ants are hunters, and live solely on insects or other prey; and it is a curious analogy that, like the hunting races of mankind, they have to change their hunting-grounds when one is exhausted, and move on to another. In Nicaragua they are generally called 'Army Ants.' One of the smaller species (*Eciton predator*) used occasionally to visit our house and swarm over the floors and walls, searching every cranny, and driving out the cockroaches and spiders, many of which were caught, pulled, bitten to pieces and carried off. The individuals of this species were of various sizes; the smallest measuring one and a quarter lines, and the largest three lines, or a quarter of an inch.

I saw many large armies of this, or a closely allied species, in the forest. My attention was generally first called to them by the twittering of some small birds, belonging to several different species, that follow the ants in the woods. On approaching, a dense body of the ants, three or four yards wide, and so numerous as to blacken the ground, would be seen moving rapidly in one direction, examining every cranny, and underneath every fallen leaf. On the flanks, and in advance of the main body, smaller columns would be pushed out. These smaller columns would generally first flush the cockroaches, grasshoppers, and spiders. The pursued insects would rapidly make off, but many, in their confusion and terror, would bound right into the midst of the main body of ants. At first the grasshopper, when it found itself in the midst of its enemies, would give vigorous leaps, with perhaps two or three of the ants clinging to its legs. Then it would stop a moment to rest, and that moment would be fatal, for the tiny foes would swarm over the prey, and after a few more ineffectual struggles it would succumb to its fate, and soon be bitten to pieces and carried off to the rear. The greatest catch of the ants was, however, when they got amongst some fallen brushwood. The cockroaches, spiders, and other insects, instead of running right away, would ascend the fallen branches and remain there, whilst the host of ants were occupying all the ground below. By-and-by up would come some of the ants, following every branch, and driving before them their prey to the ends of the small twigs, when nothing remained for them but to leap, and they would alight in the very throng of their foes, with the result of being certainly caught and pulled to pieces. Many of the spiders would escape by hanging suspended by a thread of silk from the branches, safe from the foes that swarmed both above and below.

I noticed that spiders generally were most intelligent in escaping, and did not, like the cockroaches and other insects, take shelter in the first hiding-place they found, only to be driven out again, or perhaps caught by the advancing army of ants. I have often seen large spiders making off many yards in advance, and apparently determined to put a good distance between themselves and the foe. I once saw one of the false spiders, or harvest-men (*Phalangidae*), standing in the midst of an army of ants, and with the greatest circumspection and coolness lifting, one after the other, its long legs, which supported its body above their reach. Sometimes as many as five out of its eight legs would be lifted at once, and whenever an ant approached one of those on which it stood, there was always a clear space within reach to put down another, so as to be able to hold up the threatened one out of danger.

I was much more surprised with the behaviour of a green, leaf-like locust. This insect stood immovably amongst a host of ants, many of which ran over its legs, without ever discovering there was food within their reach. So fixed was its instinctive knowledge that its safety depended on its immovability, that it allowed me to pick it up and replace it amongst the ants without making a single effort to escape. This species closely resembles a green leaf, and the other senses, which in the Ecitons appear to be more acute than that of sight, must have been completely deceived. It might easily have escaped from the ants by using its wings, but it would only have fallen into as great a danger, for the numerous birds that accompany the army ants are ever on the outlook for any insect that may fly up, and the heavy flying locusts, grasshoppers and cockroaches have no chance of escape. Several species of ant-thrushes always accompany the army ants in the forest. They do not, however, feed on the ants, but on the insects they disturb. Besides the ant-thrushes, trogons, creepers, and a variety of other birds, are often seen on the branches of trees above where an ant army is foraging below, pursuing and catching the insects that fly up.

The insects caught by the ants are dismembered, and their too bulky bodies bitten to pieces and carried off to the rear; and behind the army there are always small columns engaged on this duty. I have followed up these columns often; generally they led to dense masses of impenetrable brushwood, but twice they led me to cracks in the ground, down which the ants dragged their prey. These habitations are only temporary, for in a few days not an ant would be seen in the neighbourhood, but all would have moved off to fresh hunting grounds.

Thomas Belt

Running

Linford Christie
European 100 m champion
and the European Indoor
200 m champion of 1986,
and the UK record holder
at 100 m. He finished
fourth in the 1987 World
Championships.

Sprints

You generally know from the word go whether or not you are a sprinter, for all those who have made the grade throughout the history of athletics have had basic, innate speed. Very rarely have distance runners or field event athletes discovered later in their careers that they have been sprinters all along - Allan Wells is a notable exception - whereas many who imagined they were sprinters have gone on to find out that they were better at another event. I discovered at about nine years of age that I was fairly good at sprinting, but even if you are sure of this, it is still best to try out other events when you are young.

Sprinters come in all different shapes and sizes, though the most successful are at least 5'8" tall. To be successful you must be dedicated and not rely on your natural ability to get you through. The history of sprinting is littered with people unsuccessful because of this.

Technique

Starting

It is very important to view the start as the first 30 metres of the race. So many youngsters consider the start to be solely what happens on the starting blocks; whereas what must be drilled into them is the pickup towards full sprinting speed over the first third of the race. The sprinter must be drilled and drilled until his starting technique is second nature to him. For many years my start was the worst aspect of my racing simply because I was not well-drilled as a youngster. A really bad start can cost you the race, especially over 100 metres, so attention to this aspect of your running is vital.

From the moment the starter calls you to take your track suit off until you are running at full speed, one word should describe your attitude of mind - CONCENTRATION! A blink of an eyelid after the command 'Set' can lose you the race. Once you are called forward, your whole mind must be focused on the job in hand - getting away first. You will have ensured that your blocks are *firmly* in place by a few trial sprint starts.

The start position

Block spacing is a matter of comfort above all. The blocks also have to be spaced so that the most effective leg drive can be obtained. For instance, blocks which are too close together can cause too much strain on the arms and fingers, especially with starters who tend to hold in that position. On the command 'On Your Marks', you move ahead of the blocks and step back into them. The rule states that the toe of the spikes must touch the ground. On average the arms should be shoulder width apart, but again this will vary from athlete to athlete. The head should be in natural alignment with the body, so that you are looking forward 20 or 30 metres down the track.

Set

On the command 'Set', your hips move into their running position and your shoulders move slightly ahead of your hands. You are steadily poised and coiled like a spring waiting for the gun. Here there must be maximum concentration; the slightest inattention can lose the race.

The gun

On the gun, drive forward from the blocks. Here all concentration must be on 'keeping low' and this is where the month-after-month, year-after-year of starting drills should pay off. Many young sprinters immediately leap up into the normal running stance as soon as the gun is fired, which cuts down on their stride length - the sensation is almost like running on the spot - and thus valuable ground and hundredths of seconds are lost.

The first 30 metres

At the gun, the lead arm is thrown forward and you aim at driving *forward*. Knee pick-up will take care of itself. Arm action throughout must concentrate on the *backward* pull, for this assists in leg drive. So, *pull the arm back* slightly bent and then get it forward as fast as possible to bring about the next pull back. The sprinter then *drives forward* and rises gradually over the first 30 metres to a full sprinting stance.

Start drills

The advice of a qualified coach is absolutely necessary in gaining a good sprint start and *this cannot be sought a moment too soon*. Many sprinters do not start being seriously coached until they are sixteen years of age and this is often too late - it certainly was in my case - for bad habits will almost certainly have set in by then. Starting drills must be part of every training programme:
1   Always over at least 50 metres (the full bend for 200 metres).
2   Always against opposition. If others in the squad are slower than you, then give them a handicap.
Other activity such as uphill running *on grass* (never on the road), sometimes pulling a tyre, is ideal in order to train the body to *keep low* over the opening phase of the race.

Starting for 200 metres

At the start of the 200 metres the sprinter is on the bend but he should aim at the outset to achieve for himself as straight a line as is possible. So he will set his blocks on the outside of the lane, aiming at a starting 'line' tangential to the outside line of the lane inside him. Before the race you should stride the bend (tracks have different radii) and then you will discover the angle at which you will approach the bend and set your blocks accordingly. It is a general rule that the further out you are in lane terms from the inside of the track, the greater will be the angle of the blocks to the line inside you.

The aim in the 200 metres is to 'run a good bend', for invariably the athlete leading into the straight turns out to be the winner.

Relaxation

The key to great sprinting is relaxation. This applies to both sprint races, but especially to the 200 metres. Once an athlete begins to strain and tie-up, his shoulders rise, his head goes back and *he starts to slow down*. Maximum speed is reached at around 60 metres. So concentration (that word again) - on relaxing, keeping the knees high, swinging the arms back in a relaxed manner to keep the momentum going - is vitally important. If you get the opportunity of studying slow-motion film of great sprinting from the front, you will see just how relaxed they are. In the 200 metres this process has to apply for a much longer period - lactic acid and general fatigue are fighting to take over after 60 metres and your battle is as much if not more with them than with the other sprinters!

In the longer race the sprinter in the lead has a big advantage, in that he can concentrate on relaxing and controlling the race whereas those behind him will tend to strain to catch up. If you are behind after the bend - like I am sometimes! - then the message is 'don't panic'. Panic creates strain and tension and you start to tie up. Just keep lifting your knees and concentrate on fast, relaxed sprinting.

It is a good maxim that the fitter you are, the more relaxed you can become.

The finish

The most important factor in finishing is that the sprinter should sprint for 110 metres or 210 metres; again this must be inculcated into the mind of the athlete. So many sprinters - even the most experienced - begin to anticipate the finish line about ten metres out and either start slowing down or begin to adopt a 'dip' finish, thus affecting their running action over the last four or five metres. Young and up-and-coming sprinters should first concentrate on sprinting *all the way through* the finish line and beyond.

Some sprinters do employ a dip finish (where the arms are thrown back and the trunk leaned excessively forward) which can win races in very close finishes. However, the timing of this technique is absolutely crucial if it is to be effective and requires constant practice. Unless a sprinter can perfect it, then he should just concentrate on maintaining good sprinting action through the line.

Linford Christie

WITNESSING

A Hanging

It was in Burma, a sodden morning of the rains. A sickly light, like yellow tinfoil, was slanting over the high walls into the jail yard. We were waiting outside the condemned cells, a row of sheds fronted with double bars, like small animal cages. Each cell measured about ten feet by ten and was quite bare within except for a plank bed and a pot for drinking water. In some of them brown, silent men were squatting at the inner bars, with their blankets draped round them. These were the condemned men, due to be hanged within the next week or two.

One prisoner had been brought out of his cell. He was a Hindu, a puny wisp of a man, with a shaven head and vague liquid eyes. He had a thick, sprouting moustache, absurdly too big for his body, rather like the moustache of a comic man on the films. Six tall Indian warders were guarding him and getting him ready for the gallows. Two of them stood by with rifles and fixed bayonets, while the others handcuffed him, passed a chain through his handcuffs and fixed it to their belts, and lashed his arms tight to his sides. They crowded very close about him, with their hands always on him in a careful, caressing grip, as though all the while feeling him to make sure he was there. It was like men handling a fish which is still alive and may jump back into the water. But he stood quite unresisting, yielding his arms limply to the ropes, as though he hardly noticed what was happening.

Eight o'clock struck and a bugle call, desolately thin in the wet air, floated from the distant barracks. The superintendent of the jail, who was standing apart from the rest of us, moodily prodding the gravel with his stick, raised his head at the sound. He was an army doctor, with a grey toothbrush moustache and a gruff voice. "For God's sake hurry up, Francis," he said irritably. "The man ought to have been dead by this time. Aren't you ready yet?"

Francis, the head jailer, a fat Dravidian in a white drill suit and gold spectacles, waved his black hand. "Yes sir, yes sir," he bubbled. "All iss satisfactorily prepared. The hangman iss waiting. We shall proceed."

"Well, quick march, then. The prisoners can't get their breakfast till this job's over."

We set out for the gallows. Two warders marched on either side of the prisoner, with their rifles at the slope; two others marched close against him, gripping him by arm and shoulder, as though at once pushing and supporting him. The rest of us, magistrates and the like, followed behind. Suddenly, when we had gone ten yards, the procession stopped short without any order or warning. A dreadful thing had happened - a dog, come goodness knows whence, had appeared in the yard. It came bounding among us with a loud volley of barks and leapt round us wagging its whole body, wild with glee at finding so many human beings together. It was a large woolly dog, half Airedale, half pariah. For a moment it pranced round us, and then, before anyone could stop it, it had made a dash for the prisoner, and jumping up tried to lick his face. Everybody stood aghast, too taken aback to even grab the dog.

"Who let that bloody brute in here?" said the superintendent angrily. "Catch it, someone!"

A warder detached from the escort, charged clumsily after the dog, but it danced and gambolled just out of his reach, taking everything as part of the game. A young Eurasian jailer picked up a handful of gravel and tried to stone the dog away, but it dodged the stones and came after us again. Its yaps echoed from the jail walls. The prisoner, in the grasp of the two warders, looked on incuriously, as though this was another formality of the hanging. It was several minutes before someone managed to catch the dog. Then we put my handkerchief through its collar and moved off once more, with the dog still straining and whimpering.

It was about forty yards to the gallows. I watched the bare brown back of the prisoner marching in front of me. He walked clumsily with his bound arms, but quite steadily, with that bobbing gait of the Indian who never straightens his knees. At each step his muscles slid neatly into place, the lock of hair on his scalp danced up and down, his feet printed themselves on the wet gravel. And once, in spite of the men who gripped him by each shoulder, he stepped lightly aside to avoid a puddle on the path.

It is curious; but till that moment I had never realized what it means to destroy a healthy, conscious man. When I saw the prisoner step aside to avoid the puddle I saw the mystery, the unspeakable wrongness, of cutting a life short when it is in full tide. This man was not dying, he was alive just as we are alive. All the organs of his body were working - bowels digesting food, skin renewing itself, nails growing, tissues forming - all toiling away in solemn foolery. His nails would still be growing when he stood on the drop, when he was falling through the air with a tenth-of-a-second to live. His eyes saw the yellow gravel and the grey walls, and his brain still remembered, foresaw, reasoned - even about puddles. He and we were a party of men walking together, seeing, hearing, feeling, understanding the same world; and in two minutes, with a sudden snap, one of us would be gone - one mind less, one world less.

The gallows stood in a small yard, separate from the main grounds of the prison, and overgrown with tall prickly weeds. It was a brick erection like three sides of a shed, with planking on top, and above that two beams and a crossbar with the rope dangling. The hangman, a greyhaired convict in the white uniform of the prison, was waiting beside his machine. He greeted us with a servile crouch as we entered. At a word from Francis the two warders, gripping the prisoner more closely than ever, half led, half pushed him to the gallows and helped him clumsily up the ladder. Then the hangman climbed up and fixed the rope round the prisoner's neck.

We stood waiting, five yards away. The warders had formed in a rough circle round the gallows. And then, when the noose was fixed, the prisoner began crying out to his god. It was a high, reiterated cry of "Ram! Ram! Ram! Ram!" not urgent and fearful like a prayer or cry for help, but steady, rhythmical, almost like the tolling of a bell. The dog answered the sound with a whine. The hangman, still standing on the gallows, produced a small cotton bag like a flourbag and drew it down over the prisoner's face. But the sound, muffled by the cloth, still persisted, over and over again: "Ram! Ram! Ram! Ram! Ram!"

The hangman climbed down and stood ready, holding the lever. Minutes seemed to pass. The steady, muffled crying from the prisoner went on and on, "Ram! Ram! Ram!" never faltering for an instant. The superintendent, his head on his chest, was slowly poking the ground with his stick; perhaps he was counting the cries, allowing the prisoner a fixed number—fifty, perhaps, or a hundred. Everyone had changed colour. The Indians had gone grey like bad coffee, and one or two of the bayonets were wavering. We looked at the lashed, hooded man on the drop, and listened to his cries - each cry another second of life; the same thought was in all our minds; oh, kill him quickly, get it over, stop that abominable noise!

Suddenly the superintendent made up his mind. Throwing up his head he made a swift motion with his stick. "Chalo!" he shouted almost fiercely.

There was a clanking noise, and then dead silence. The prisoner had vanished, and the rope was twisting on itself. I let go of the dog, and it galloped immediately to the back of the gallows; but when it got there it stopped short, barked, and then retreated into a corner of the yard, where it stood among the weeds, looking timorously out at us. We went round the gallows to inspect the prisoner's body. He was dangling with his toes pointed straight downwards, very slowly revolving, as dead as a stone.

The superintendent reached out with his stick and poked the bare brown body; it oscillated slightly. *"He's* all right," said the superintendent. He backed out from under the gallows, and blew out a deep breath. The moody look had gone out of his face quite suddenly. He glanced at his wrist-watch. "Eight minutes past eight. Well, that's all for this morning, thank God."

The warders unfixed bayonets and marched away. The dog, sobered and conscious of having misbehaved itself, slipped after them. We walked out of the gallows yard, past the condemned cells with their waiting prisoners, into the big central yard of the prison. The convicts, under the command of warders armed with lathis, were already receiving their breakfast. They squatted in long rows, each man holding a tin pannikin, while two warders with buckets marched round ladling out rice; it seemed quite a homely, jolly scene, after the hanging. An enormous relief had come upon us now that the job was done. One felt an impulse to sing, to break into a run, to snigger. All at once everyone began chattering gaily.

The Eurasian boy walking beside me nodded towards the way we had come, with a knowing smile: "Do you know, sir, our friend (he meant the dead man) when he heard his appeal had been dismissed, he pissed on the floor of his cell. From fright. Kindly take one of my cigarettes, sir. Do you not admire my new silver case, sir? From the boxwallah, two rupees eight annas. Classy European style."

Several people laughed - at what, nobody seemed certain.

Francis was walking by the superintendent, talking garrulously: "Well, sir, all has passed off with the utmost satisfactoriness. It was all finished - flick! Like that. It iss not always so—oah, no! I have known cases where the doctor wass obliged to go beneath the gallows and pull the prissoner's legs to ensure decease. Most disagreeable!"

"Wriggling about, eh? That's bad," said the superintendent.

"Arch, sir, it iss worse when they become refractory! One man, I recall, clung to the bars of hiss cage when we went to take him out. You will scarcely credit, sir, that it took six warders to dislodge him, three pulling at each leg. We reasoned with him, "My dear fellow," we said, "think of all the pain and trouble you are causing to us!" But no, he would not listen! Ach, he wass very troublesome!"

I found that I was laughing quite loudly. Everyone was laughing. Even the superintendent grinned in a tolerant way. "You'd better all come out and have a drink," he said quite genially. "I've got a bottle of whisky in the car. We could do with it."

We went through the big double gates of the prison into the road. "Pulling at his legs!" exclaimed a Burmese magistrate suddenly, and burst into a loud chuckling. We all began laughing again. At that moment Francis' anecdote seemed extraordinarily funny. We all had a drink together, native and European alike, quite amicably. The dead man was a hundred yards away.

George Orwell

The Arrest of Dr Crippen

Wife-murderer Crippen was the first criminal to be hunted down by wireless. He was executed, but Ethel le Neve, charged as an accessory, was acquitted. The narrator is Captain Kendall, master of the Canadian Pacific liner Montrose.

The *Montrose* was in port at Antwerp when I read in the *Continental Daily Mail* that a warrant had been issued for Crippen and le Neve. They were reported to have been traced to a hotel in Brussels but had then vanished again.

Soon after we sailed for Quebec I happened to glance through the porthole of my cabin and behind a lifeboat I saw two men. One was squeezing the other's hand. I walked along the boat deck and got into conversation with the elder man. I noticed that there was a mark on the bridge of his nose through wearing spectacles, that he had recently shaved off a moustache, and that he was growing a beard. The young fellow was very reserved, and I remarked about his cough.

"Yes," said the elder man, "my boy has a weak chest, and I'm taking him to California for his health."

I returned to my cabin and had another look at the *Daily Mail*. I studied the description and photographs issued by Scotland Yard. Crippen was 50 years of age, 5 ft 4 ins high, wearing spectacles and a moustache; Miss le Neve was 27, 5 ft 5 ins, slim, with pale complexion. I then examined the passenger list and ascertained that the two passengers were travelling as 'Mr Robinson and son'. I arranged for them to take meals at my table.

When the bell went for lunch I tarried until the coast was clear, then slipped into the Robinsons' cabin unobserved, where I noticed two things: that the boy's felt hat was packed round the rim to make it fit, and that he had been using a piece of a woman's bodice as a face flannel. That satisfied me. I went down to the dining saloon and kept my eyes open. The boy's manners at table were ladylike. Later, when they were promenading the saloon deck, I went out and walked behind them, and called out, "Mr Robinson!" I had to shout the name several times before the man turned and said to me, "I'm sorry, Captain, I didn't hear you - this cold wind is making me deaf."

In the next two days we developed our acquaintance. Mr Robinson was the acme of politeness, quiet-mannered, a non-smoker; at night he went on deck and roamed about on his own. Once the wind blew up his coat tails and in his hip pocket I saw a revolver. After that I also carried a revolver, and we often had pleasant little tea parties together in my cabin, discussing the book he was reading, which was *The Four Just Men*, a murder mystery by Edgar Wallace - and when that little fact was wirelessed to London and published it made Edgar Wallace's name ring, so agog was everybody in England over the Crippen case.

That brings me to the wireless. On the third day out I gave my wireless operator a message for Liverpool: *One hundred and thirty miles west of Lizard ... have strong suspicions that Crippen London cellar murderer and accomplice are among saloon passengers ... Accomplice dressed as boy; voice, manner, and build undoubtedly a girl.*

I remember Mr Robinson sitting in a deckchair, looking at the wireless aerials and listening to the crackling of our crude spark-transmitter, and remarking to me what a wonderful invention it was.

I sent several more reports, but our weak transmitting apparatus was soon out of communication with land. We could hear other ships at a great distance, however, and you may imagine my excitement when my operator brought me a message he had intercepted from a London newspaper to its representative aboard the White Star liner *Laurentic* which was also heading westward across the Atlantic: *What is Inspector Dew doing? Is he sending and receiving wireless messages? Is he playing games with passengers? Are passengers excited over chase? Rush reply.*

This was the first I knew that my message to Liverpool had caused Inspector Dew to catch the first boat out - the *Laurentic*. With her superior speed I knew she would reach the Newfoundland coast before me. I hoped that if she had any news for me the *Laurentic* would leave it at the Belle Island station to be transmitted to me as soon as I passed that point on my approach to Canada.

She had news indeed: *Will board you at Father Point ... strictly confidential ... from Inspector Dew, Scotland Yard, on board* Laurentic.

I replied: *Shall arrive Father Point about 6 a.m. tomorrow . . . should advise you to come off in small boat with pilot, disguised as pilot ... .*

This was confirmed. The last night was dreary and anxious, the sound of our fog-horn every few minutes adding to the monotony. The hours dragged on as I paced the bridge; now and then I could see Mr Robinson strolling about the deck. I had invited him to get up early to see the 'pilots' come aboard at Father Point in the River St Lawrence. When they did so they came straight to my cabin. I sent for Mr Robinson. When he entered I stood with the detective facing the door, holding my revolver inside my coat pocket. As he came in, I said, "Let me introduce you."

Mr Robinson put out his hand, the detective grabbed it, at the same time removing his pilot's cap, and said, "Good morning, Dr Crippen. Do you know me? I'm Inspector Dew, from Scotland Yard."

Crippen quivered. Surprise struck him dumb. Then he said, "Thank God it's over. The suspense has been too great. I couldn't stand it any longer."

Captain H. G. Kendall

Not My Best Side

I

Not my best side, I'm afraid.
The artist didn't give me a chance to
Pose properly, and as you can see,
Poor chap, he had this obsession with
Triangles, so he left off two of my
Feet. I didn't comment at the time
(What, after all, are two feet
To a monster?) but afterwards
I was sorry for the bad publicity.
Why, I said to myself, should my conqueror
Be so ostentatiously beardless, and ride
A horse with a deformed neck and square hoofs?
Why should my victim be so

Unattractive as to be inedible,
And why should she have me literally
On a string? I don't mind dying
Ritually, since I always rise again,
But I should have liked a little more blood
To show they were taking me seriously.

II

It's hard for a girl to be sure if
She wants to be rescued. I mean, I quite
Took to the dragon. It's nice to be
Liked, if you know what I mean. He was
So nicely physical, with his claws
And lovely green skin, and that sexy tail,
And the way he looked at me,
He made me feel he was all ready to
Eat me. And any girl enjoys that.
So when this boy turned up, wearing machinery,
On a really *dangerous* horse, to be honest,
I didn't much fancy him. I mean,

St George and the Dragon, What was he like underneath the hardware?
Paolo Uccello He might have acne, blackheads or even

Bad breath for all I could tell, but the dragon -
Well, you could see all his equipment
At a glance. Still, what could I do?
The dragon got himself beaten by the boy,
And a girl's got to think of her future.

III
I have diplomas in Dragon
Management and Virgin Reclamation.
My horse is the latest model, with
Automatic transmission and built-in
Obsolescence. My spear is custom-built,
And my prototype armour
Still on the secret list. You can't
Do better than me at the moment.
I'm qualified and equipped to the
Eyebrow. So why be difficult?
Don't you want to be killed and/or rescued
In the most contemporary way? Don't
You want to carry out the roles
That sociology and myth have designed for you?
Don't you realize that, by being choosy,
You are endangering job-prospects
In the spear- and horse-building industries?
What, in any case, does it matter what
You want? You're in my way.

U. A. Fanthorpe

The Cry

Once in the grass
there lived a nervous insect,
the tiniest creature in the whole wide world.
He'd been afraid of the wind all his life
and so, to get away from it,
he dug a hole, sweating and panting.
It took a year to do.

Once in the hole
he was cowering happily, when
the gentlest zephyr in the whole wide world
fanned softly
and blew a tiny bit of earth into the hole.
The insect, uttering
the smallest saddest cry in the whole wide world
expired.

Amano Tadashi

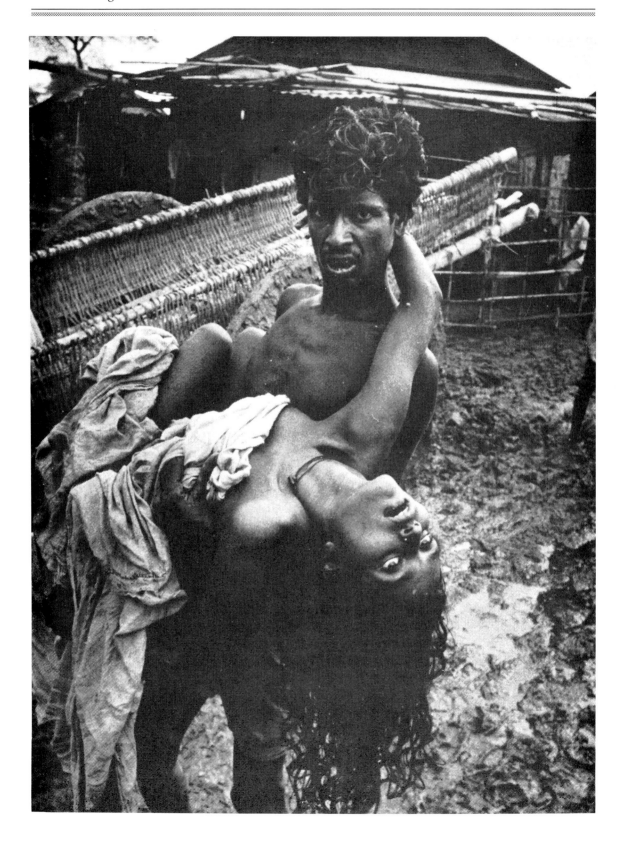

A Life in Pictures

All my photography is confrontation. I did not happen to come across this man with his wife in his arms. I was not in their country by chance. I took this shot because I went there: to stick it up the nose of the person looking at this picture who has more of everything than the woman who was dying. I went to Bangladesh and was so humiliated and horrified and sickened by what I saw that I just kept shooting. I saw people dying in the mud, and parents crying over their dead children. I was so moved and so heartbroken that I couldn't possibly stop. Nobody, I thought, is going to get a free ride out of me. They're going to look at these people suffering.

This photograph is like a lot of others I take. I'm trying to shoot them so that you can't escape looking: they force themselves on you. If anything, I'm trying to photograph in the way that Goya painted or did his war sketches. I'm trying to bring in the surroundings, focussed by this terrible subject. I'm hoping to show the circumstances, the cause, the source, so that there's a story to the photograph. I sometimes think of pictures as 'pictures' in the old sense: as icons, with the impact of a religious image or a ritual tragedy. In this photograph, the man is rushing off to hospital with his wife, who has advanced cholera. It's hard to get away from it. It tells you too much. I'd like to think that it sticks in your mind the way an icon does, that it's remembered the way an icon is remembered.

Don McCullin

Living Jim Crow

My first lesson in how to live as a Negro came when I was quite small. We were living in Arkansas. Our house stood behind the railroad tracks. Its skimpy yard was paved with black cinders. Nothing green ever grew in that yard. The only touch of green we could see was far away, beyond the tracks, over where the white folks lived. But cinders were good enough for me and I never missed the green growing things. And anyhow cinders were fine weapons. You could always have a nice hot war with huge black cinders. All you had to do was crouch behind the brick pillars of a house with your hands full of gritty ammunition. And the first woolly black head you saw pop out from behind another row of pillars was your target. You tried your very best to knock it off. It was great fun.

I never fully realized the appalling disadvantages of a cinder environment till one day the gang to which I belonged found itself engaged in a war with the white boys who lived beyond the tracks. As usual we laid down our cinder barrage, thinking that this would wipe the white boys out. But they replied with a steady bombardment of broken bottles. We doubled our cinder barrage, but they hid behind trees, hedges, and the sloping embankments of their lawns. Having no such fortifications, we retreated to the brick pillars of our homes. During the retreat a broken milk bottle caught me behind the ear, opening a deep gash which bled profusely. The sight of blood pouring over my face completely demoralized our ranks. My fellow-combatants left me standing paralyzed in the center of the yard, and scurried for their homes. A kind neighbor saw me and rushed me to a doctor, who took three stitches in my neck.

I sat brooding on my front steps, nursing my wound and waiting for my mother to come from work. I felt that a grave injustice had been done me. It was all right to throw cinders. The greatest harm a cinder could do was leave a bruise. But broken bottles were dangerous; they left you cut, bleeding, and helpless.

When night fell, my mother came from the white folks' kitchen. I raced down the street to meet her. I could just feel in my bones that she would understand. I knew she would tell me exactly what to do next time. I grabbed her hand and babbled out the whole story. She examined my wound, then slapped me.

"How come yuh didn't hide?" she asked me. "How come yuh awways fightin'?"

I was outraged, and bawled. Between sobs I told her that I didn't have any trees or hedges to hide behind. There wasn't a thing I could have used as a trench. And you couldn't throw very far when you were hiding behind the brick pillars of a house. She grabbed a barrel stave, dragged me home, stripped me naked, and beat me till I had a fever of one hundred and two. She would smack my rump with the stave, and while the skin was still smarting, impart to me gems of Jim Crow wisdom. I was never to throw cinders any more. I was never to fight any more wars. I was never, never, under any conditions, to fight *white* folks again. And they were absolutely right in clouting me with the broken milk bottle. Didn't I know she was working hard every day in the hot kitchens of the white folks to make money to take care of me? When was I ever going to learn to be a good boy? She couldn't be bothered with my fights. She finished by telling me that I ought to be thankful to God as long as I lived that they didn't kill me.

All that night I was delirious and could not sleep. Each time I closed my eyes I saw monstrous white faces suspended from the ceiling, leering at me.

From that time on, the charm of my cinder yard was gone. The green trees, the trimmed hedges, the cropped lawns grew very meaningful, became a symbol. Even today when I think of white folks, the hard, sharp outlines of white houses surrounded by trees, lawns, and hedges are present somewhere in the background of my mind. Through the years they grew to an overreaching symbol of fear.

It was a long time before I came in close contact with white folks again. We moved from Arkansas to Mississippi. Here we had the good fortune not to live behind the railroad tracks, or close to white neighborhoods. We lived in the very heart of the local Black Belt. There were black churches and black preachers; there were black schools and black teachers, black groceries and black clerks. In fact, everything was so solidly black that for a long time I did not even think of white folks, save in remote and vague terms. But this could not last forever. As one grows older one eats more. One's clothing costs more. When I finished grammar school I had to go to work. My mother could no longer feed and clothe me on her cooking job.

There is only one place where a black boy who knows no trade can get a job, and that's where the houses and faces are white, where the trees, lawns, and hedges are green. My first job was with an optical company in Jackson, Mississippi. The morning I applied I stood straight and neat before the boss, answering all his questions with sharp yessirs and nosirs. I was very careful to pronounce my *sirs* distinctly, in order that he might know that I was polite, that I knew where I was, and that I knew he was a *white* man. I wanted that job badly.

He looked me over as though he were examining a prize poodle. He questioned me closely about my schooling, being particularly insistent about how much mathematics I had had. He seemed very pleased when I told him I had had two years of algebra.

"Boy, how would you like to learn something around here?" he asked me.

"I'd like it fine, sir," I said, happy. I had visions of 'working my way up.' Even Negroes have those visions.

"All right," he said. "Come on."

I followed him to the small factory.

"Pease," he said to a white man of about thirty-five, "this is Richard. He's going to work for us."

Pease looked at me and he nodded.

I was then taken to a white boy of about seventeen.

"Morrie, this is Richard, who's going to work for us."

"Whut yuh sayin' there, boy!" Morrie boomed at me.

"Fine!" I answered.

The boss instructed these two to help me, teach me, give me jobs to do, and let me learn what I could in my spare time.

My wages were five dollars a week.

I worked hard, trying to please. For the first month I got along O.K. Both Pease and Morrie seemed to like me. But one thing was missing. And I kept on thinking about it. I was not learning anything and nobody was volunteering to help me. Thinking they had forgotten that I was to learn something about the mechanics of grinding lenses, I asked Morrie one day to tell me about the work. He grew red.

"Whut yuh tryin' t' do, nigger, get smart?" he asked.

"Naw; I ain' tryin' t' git smart," I said.

"Well, don't, if yuh know whut's good for yuh!"

I was puzzled. Maybe he just doesn't want to help me, I thought. I went to Pease.

"Say, are yuh crazy, you black bastard?" Pease asked me, his gray eyes growing hard.

I spoke out, reminding him that the boss had said I was to be given a chance to learn something.

"Nigger, you think you're *white*, don't you?"

"Naw, sir!"

"Well, you're acting mighty like it!"

"But, Mr Pease, the boss said . . ."

Pease shook his fist in my face.

"This is a *white* man's work around here, and you better watch yourself!"

From then on they changed toward me. They said good-morning no more. When I was a bit slow performing some duty, I was called a lazy black son-of-a-bitch.

Once I thought of reporting all this to the boss. But the mere idea of what would happen to me if Pease and Morrie should learn that I had 'snitched' stopped me. And after all the boss was a white man, too. What was the use?

The climax came at noon one summer day. Pease called me to his work-bench. To get to him I had to go between two narrow benches and stand with my back against a wall.

"Yes, sir," I said.

"Richard, I want to ask you something," Pease began pleasantly, not looking up from his work.

"Yes, sir," I said again.

Morrie came over, blocking the narrow passage between the benches. He folded his arms, staring at me solemnly.

I looked from one to the other, sensing that something was coming.

"Yes, sir," I said for the third time.

Pease looked up and spoke very slowly.

"Richard, *Mr* Morrie here tells me you called me *Pease*."

I stiffened. A void seemed to open up in me. I knew this was the show-down.

He meant that I had failed to call him Mr Pease. I looked at Morrie. He was gripping a steel bar in his hands. I opened my mouth to speak, to protest, to assure Pease that I had never called him simply *Pease* and that I had never had any intentions of doing so, when Morrie grabbed me by the collar, ramming my head against the wall.

"Now, be careful, nigger!" snarled Morrie, baring his teeth. "*I* heard yuh call 'im *Pease!* 'N' if you say yuh didn't, yuh're callin' me a *lie*, see?" He waved the steel bar threateningly.

If I had said: No sir, Mr Pease, I never called you *Pease*, I would have been automatically calling Morrie a liar. And if I had said: Yes sir Mr Pease, I called you *Pease*, I would have been pleading guilty to having uttered the worst insult that a Negro can utter to a southern

The news agency information attached to the photograph:

THE SOUTH VERSUS THE FEDERAL GOVERNMENT

LITTLE ROCK, ARK.: Hazel Bryant (center background
with mouth open) shouts epithets at Negro girl
student Elizabeth Eckford, as the Eckford girl tries
to pass through the lines of National Guardsmen (in
this photo made 9/6/57) in an effort to gain
entrance to Little Rock's Central High School.

white man. I stood hesitating, trying to frame a neutral reply.

"Richard, I asked you a question!" said Pease. Anger was creeping into his voice.

"I don't remember calling you *Pease*, Mr Pease," I said cautiously. "And if I did, I'm sure I didn't mean . . ."

"You black son-of-a-bitch! You called me *Pease*, then!" he spat, slapping me sideways over a bench. Morrie was on top of me, demanding:

"Didn't yuh call 'im *Pease*? If yuh say yuh didn't I'll rip yo' gut string loose with this bar, yuh black granny dodger! Yuh can't call a white man a lie 'n' git erway with it, you black son-of-a-bitch!"

I wilted. I begged them not to bother me. I knew what they wanted. They wanted me to leave.

"I'll leave," I promised. "I'll leave right *now*."

They gave me a minute to get out of the factory. I was warned not to show up again, or tell the boss.

I went.

When I told the folks at home what had happened, they called me a fool. They told me I must never again attempt to exceed my boundaries. When you are working for white folks, they said, you got to 'stay in your place' if you want to keep working.

Richard Wright

The Amateur Scientist

When I was a kid I had a 'lab.' It wasn't a laboratory in the sense that I would measure, or do important experiments. Instead, I would play: I'd make a motor, I'd make a gadget that would go off when something passed a photocell, I'd play around with selenium; I was piddling around all the time. I did calculate a little bit for the lamp bank, a series of switches and bulbs I used as resistors to control voltages. But all that was for application. I never did any laboratory kind of experiments.

I also had a microscope and *loved* to watch things under the microscope. It took patience: I would get something under the microscope and I would watch it interminably. I saw many interesting things, like everybody sees - a diatom slowly making its way across the slide, and so on.

One day I was watching a paramecium and I saw something that was not described in the books I got in school - in college, even. These books always simplify things so the world will be more like *they* want it to be: When they're talking about the behavior of animals, they always start out with, 'The paramecium is extremely simple; it has a simple behavior. It turns as its slipper shape moves through the water until it hits something, at which time it recoils, turns through an angle, and then starts out again.'

It isn't really right. First of all, as everybody knows, the paramecia, from time to time, conjugate with each other - they meet and exchange nuclei. How do they decide when it's time to do that? (Never mind; that's not my observation.)

I watched these paramecia hit something, recoil, turn through an angle, and go again. The idea that it's mechanical, like a computer program - it doesn't look that way. They go different distances, they recoil different distances, they turn through angles that are different in various cases; they don't always turn to the right; they're very irregular. It looks random, because you don't know what they're hitting; you don't know all the chemicals they're smelling, or what.

One of the things I wanted to watch was what happens to the paramecium when the water that it's in dries up. It was claimed that the paramecium can dry up into a sort of hardened seed. I had a drop of water on the slide under my microscope, and in the drop of water was a paramecium and some 'grass' - at the scale of the paramecium, it looked like a network of jackstraws. As the drop of water evaporated, over a time of fifteen or twenty minutes, the paramecium got into a tighter and tighter situation: there was more and more of this back-and-forth until it could hardly move. It was stuck between these 'sticks,' almost jammed.

Then I saw something I had never seen or heard of: the paramecium lost its shape. It could flex itself, like an amoeba. It began to push itself against one of the sticks, and began dividing into two prongs until the division was about halfway up the paramecium, at which time it decided *that* wasn't a very good idea, and backed away.

So my impression of these animals is that their behavior is much too simplified in the books. It is not so utterly mechanical or one-dimensional as they say. They should describe the behavior of these simple animals correctly. Until we see how many dimensions of behavior even a one-celled animal has, we won't be able to fully understand the behavior of more complicated animals.

I also enjoyed watching bugs. I had an insect book when I was about thirteen. It said that dragonflies are not harmful; they don't sting. In our neighborhood it was well known that 'darning needles,' as we called them, were very dangerous when they'd sting. So if we were outside somewhere playing baseball, or something, and one of these things would fly around, everybody would run for cover, waving their arms, yelling, "A darning needle! A darning needle!"

So one day I was on the beach, and I'd just read this book that said dragonflies don't sting. A darning needle came along, and everybody was screaming and running around, and I just sat there. "Don't worry!" I said. "Darning needles don't sting!"

The thing landed on my foot. Everybody was yelling and it was a big mess, because this darning needle was sitting on my foot. And there I was, this scientific wonder, saying it wasn't going to sting me.

You're *sure* this is a story that's going to come out that it stings me - but it didn't. The book was right. But I did sweat a bit.

I also had a little hand microscope. It was a toy microscope, and I pulled the magnification piece out of it, and would hold it in my hand like a magnifying glass, even though it was a microscope of forty or fifty power. With care you could hold the focus. So I could go around and look at things right out in the street.

When I was in graduate school at Princeton, I once took it out of my pocket to look at some ants that were crawling around on some ivy. I had to exclaim out loud, I was so excited. What I saw was an ant and an aphid, which ants take care of - they carry them from plant to plant if the plant they're on is dying. In return the ants get partially digested aphid juice, called 'honeydew.' I knew that; my father had told me about it, but I had never seen it.

So here was this aphid and sure enough, an ant came along, and patted it with its feet - all around the aphid, pat, pat, pat, pat, pat. This was terribly exciting! Then the juice came out of the back of the aphid. And because it was magnified, it looked like a big, beautiful, glistening ball, like a balloon, because of the surface tension. Because the microscope wasn't very good, the drop was colored a little bit from chromatic aberration in the lens - it was a gorgeous thing!

The ant took this ball in its two front feet, lifted it off the aphid, and *held* it. The world is so different at that scale that you can pick up water and hold it! The ants probably have a fatty or greasy material on their legs that doesn't break the surface tension of the water when they hold it up. Then the ant broke the surface of the drop with its mouth, and the surface tension collapsed the drop right into his gut. It was *very* interesting to see this whole thing happen!

Richard Feynman

MAKING

Making Your Own Chocolate

In these times of economic hardship and worker alienation, perhaps you might consider growing, harvesting, and producing your own chocolate instead of relying on some huge, impersonal manufacturer. Here is how:

To grow the beans
You will need:
  1 small plantation
  4000 or so cacao seedlings
  Time

Instructions:
1 Move to within 20° N or S of the Equator (on dry land).
2 For each 5lbs. of chocolate desired per year, plant 1 cacao seedling, locating each in the shade of a larger tree (banana, mango. etc.). Plant at a density of approx. 1000 trees per hectare.
3 Wait 5-8 years for the trees to mature.

Now you are ready to harvest.

To harvest the beans
You will need:
  50 long-handled pod-whoppers
  25 machetes
  390 fermenting trays with burlap
  Help

Instructions:
1 Using your long-handled pod-whoppers, gather all ripe pods.
DO NOT CLIMB THE TREES.
2 Gently split the pods open with the machetes. Scoop out the beans.

3 Put the beans in trays in a draught-free area and cover with burlap. Let stand until the beans have turned medium brown (approx. 1 week).
4 Dry the beans in the sun, stirring occasionally until their moisture content is below 7% (approx. 3 days).

You are now ready to make chocolate. (Or to sell out the whole operation to some huge, impersonal manufacturer.)

To make chocolate liquor

You will need:
  1 cleaning machine
  1 scale
  1 roaster
  1 cracker and fanner
  1 grinding mill
  Endurance

Instructions:
1 Pass the beans through your cleaning machine to remove dried pulp and other extraneous matter.
2 Weigh, select and blend the beans as desired.

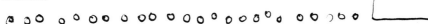

3 Roast the beans at 250°F for 2 hours.
4 Use your cracker and fanner to remove the shells from the beans, leaving the nibs.
5 Crush the nibs in your mill. The heat generated will liquefy the pulp, creating your chocolate 'mass.'

You now have the base raw material of all chocolate.

Take a vacation.

Sandra Boynton

Electrics

All householders should get to know a little about what electricity is, how it gets into our homes and how it works for us. By means of a button or switch, electricity can cook a meal or wash our clothes, so what we're talking about is a source of energy. That energy is available to every one of us via the national electricity grid system all over the UK. It is brought to our homes either by an overhead cable or by cables hidden underground. Somewhere in the house, usually near the front door, is the electricity company's main cable and main fuse. Adjacent to these will be a consumer unit (or fuse box) and a trip switch. A number of wires or cables from the consumer unit take the electricity supply around the house.

If something goes wrong with the electricity supply, lights go out, the kettle doesn't boil or the radio doesn't work. Most people's reaction is 'Oh, a fuse has blown', so a fuse is replaced and the power is switched back on. The lights, however, could go out again! The reason is simple: the fault is still there and it's imperative that the fault is traced.

To many people, electricity is something of a mystery and something that they fear: unless you know what you're doing, electricity can be dangerous. So it's the duty of all householders to get to know something about it. Ask yourself these questions. Do you really know how to wire a plug correctly? Do you know the correct colour coding? Do you know the correct fuse for different appliances? Are you aware that outside lights need special fittings and do you know about continuity testers? This all adds up to awareness of the fundamental principles of electricity.

Perhaps strangely, all the work that electricity does is the result of 'pressure'. Pressure, in electrical terms, is called the 'voltage', and is exerted by the supply. For example, 2 volts, which is what a torch battery gives, produces a small light, whereas the 240 volts mains supply will light up the whole house. It is also the pressure, or number of volts, in the supply that can cause problems if something goes wrong. No harm comes to you if you touch a 2-volt battery, but an accident with 240 volts can be dangerous. Treating electricity with circumspection means that you will become more aware of what you can and cannot do when dealing with wires, sockets and appliances. Think of it this way: electricity flows through wires; if something goes wrong, the very first thing that you must do is stop the flow. First at the nearest power point or socket and then at the consumer unit or fuse box. If a person accidentally touches a live wire, the electricity will flow through that person causing a shock, in which case you'd switch off the flow, or supply, immediately. The alternative is to remove the person from the electricity supply, using something that is non-conducting. You should always remember that metal and water (or wet materials) are very good conductors of electricity, so never use anything metallic or damp near live electricity.

The electricity supply to your home is the electricity company's responsibility as far as the beginning of your own installation; near to your consumer unit is their sealed main fuse. From your consumer unit, wires and cables of different thicknesses carry the supply to the various outlets in the house. The 1 mm cable supplies all the lighting points, whilst a 2.5 mm one runs to all the power sockets. Heavier

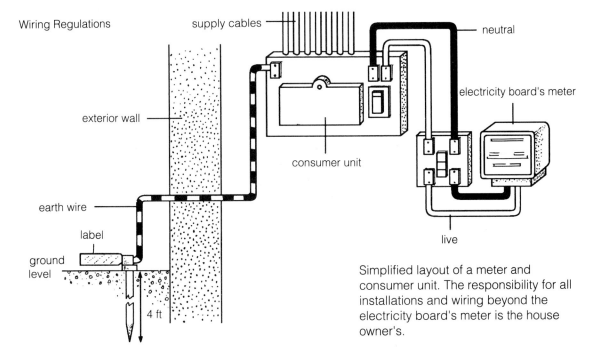

Wiring Regulations

Simplified layout of a meter and consumer unit. The responsibility for all installations and wiring beyond the electricity board's meter is the house owner's.

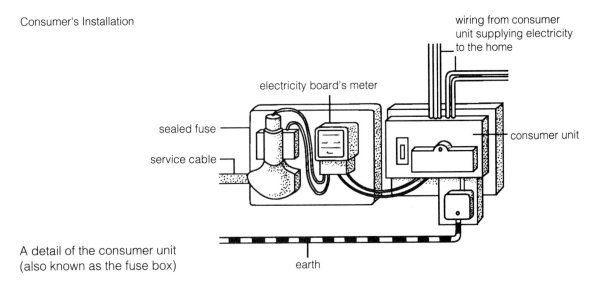

Consumer's Installation

A detail of the consumer unit (also known as the fuse box)

cables are used for such things as cookers.

Probably the most important factor in any electrical installation is 'earthing' and this is our own responsibility. It is a safety factor. Should a fault occur in the circuit, the cause could be damage to a cable: perhaps a nail or a screw has pierced a cable through a floorboard or into a wall. First of all, check all appliances, especially plug connections; check connections in ceiling roses and connections behind wall lights and flexes. You must, of course, switch off the source of the power at the fuse box before dealing with any fault.

The Institute of Electrical Engineers has produced a book which every householder should have handy: a clearly-illustrated 'Guide to Electricity'. It's written by experts but in layman's terms. It tells you, the householder, what you can do with electricity and how to do it.

Probably the simplest electrical job that you'll have to tackle is putting a new fuse in a plug. It's simple, but it's also vitally important, for your safety and for the appliance, to fit the correctly-rated fuse. Electric blankets, tape recorders, clocks, and lighting up to 720 watts need a 3 amp fuse, whereas electric irons, fires, washing machines and fridges need a 13 amp fuse. Always follow the instructions carefully. Never ever be tempted to use anything other than the correct fuse. And if you have any doubts when dealing with electricity, consult an electrician.

Fitting a fuse
Remove the plug cover by removing the central screw. Lever out the cartridge fuse and try not to disturb the clips. Whilst the cover is off, first of all check that all the screws holding the wires in the terminals are tight. Check that the plastic sheathing covering the wires meets the terminals. Check that all the wires are safely housed inside the terminals. Make sure that the outer covering of the wire is held securely by the cord-clip. Now push the correctly-rated cartridge fuse into the two holders and refit the cover.

Wiring a plug
Some older houses might still have socket outlets or power points which take round-end plugs. However, houses built in the last forty years will certainly have been wired with 'ring-main' circuits and the sockets will be single or dual 13 amp outlets with rectangular holes. These take the more common plug which has three flat pins. Whilst wiring the plug, make certain that the fuse is correctly rated. Your television set and possibly your vacuum cleaner could be rated at less than 720 watts, so you might think that a 3 amp fuse is sufficient, but appliances of this nature require a high starting current and the manufacturers recommend a 13 amp fuse. Check the recommended rating every time you wire a plug or replace a fuse.

Always go to a reputable electrical showroom or store to buy your plugs. Poor quality plugs give poor service and could cause problems. The pins can move and cause bad connections and overheating.

Get to know, and understand, the colour code first. Remove about 2 inches (5 cm) of the outer insulation without cutting into the coloured insulation covering the flex. The colour code of the flex is standard. Brown or red is live, blue or black is neutral and green or yellow and green is earth.

After you have removed the cover of the plug, the earth terminal will be at the top of the plug with the clamp at the bottom. The 'live' terminal marked 'L' is on the right near the cartridge fuse and the 'neutral' terminal marked 'N' is on the left. Pop the wires underneath the clamp so that it secures the outer insulation. Your plug may have a 'V' shaped grip, in which to force the outer insulation. You'll see that it is then clamped and cannot be pulled out. Lay each wire as far as its appropriate terminal and carefully remove the insulation with wire strippers or a sharp knife. The insulation must not be short of the terminals and there must be no straggling wires! Allow about 0.5 inch (1 cm) of bare wire to go into the terminal. If your plug has clamp type terminals, unscrew them to wind the wires round the terminal posts in a clockwise direction. Then replace the screw. You will have wired blue to the neutral terminal, brown to the live terminal and yellow and green to the earth. Make a second check before replacing the cover.

When you buy a new plug, you'll find a cartridge fuse inside it, probably a 13 amp. Don't automatically think that this fuse is the correctly rated one for your fitting. If you put that onto a metal table-lamp which then goes wrong, you won't have the protection that you should. A light fitting must have a 3 amp fuse in its plug.

Safety points

1 When dealing with any electrical appliance or electrical connections, whether you are carrying out an investigation or just checking, remember the all-important rule of making it safe by first switching off the power.

2 If the fault is with the electric appliance, switch off the appliance at the socket and pull out the plug. Remember this too: the fault may be in the switch itself, so don't depend upon switching off to make it safe.

3 If an emergency occurs and the lights have gone out, make sure that your repair kit is handy. In the kit should be a couple of screwdrivers, a torch, a pair of pliers, a trimming knife and spare fuses.

4 Never load an adaptor with another adaptor and try to run four or five appliances from it.

5 If you can't get the pins of a plug into a socket, don't try to open up the socket with something like a steel knitting needle!

6 Always keep a chemical fire-extinguisher handy in the house.

Never use water to put out a fire in an electrical appliance.

7 Extension cords and flexes should never be trailed over radiators or heating pipes. The insulation could dry out, crack and cause a short-circuit.

8 The lighting circuit must only be used for lights. Never change the plug fitting of an appliance to use it in the lighting circuit.

9 Lightning has to go to earth somewhere. Being high up, television aerials are particularly vulnerable. Switch off your set during a thunderstorm.

10 If you want to change the shade on a table lamp, wait until it's completely cool: a lot of heat is generated around the fitting. It can become difficult to unscrew, but take out the plug (as *always* when dealing with light fittings) and take your time.

11 If you have a test screwdriver that is activated by holding your finger onto a metal button, treat it with caution. Should it be faulty in any way at all, *you* will be the conductor of electricity.

12 Wire-strippers will do their job efficiently virtually unaided, so don't pull at the insulation. Always measure carefully the amount of insulation you need to remove: none of the wire should show outside the terminal when the connection is made. Lastly, when stripping flex of its insulation, take care not to sever any of the fine strands. The gauge of the flex will be reduced and therefore also its current capacity.

Harry Greene

How to Kill a Bull at a Fiesta

The brave fiesta, also called the most artistic and cruel way of killing an animal, consists of six performances in which six bulls are killed by three bullfighters, one at a time. Each of these individual performances consists of three main parts whose continuity presents one of the most beautiful and bloody spectacles which people pay to watch during the sunny afternoon in Spain and certain countries in Latin America.

The first part, called *tanteo*, begins with the sound of the trumpet, which is the signal for the doors to be opened to let the imposing beast in. The matador's aids receive the animal with their capes and make him attack and move in different directions, thus allowing the matador to observe the characteristics and peculiarities of the bull. While observing, the matador is mentally preparing his strategy for that particular bull. Once the bullfighter has completed his observing, he walks towards the bull and verifies with his cape if his ideas about the animal were accurate or wrong, and at the same time he modifies, if necessary, his original strategy. Next, the bull is driven to the picador, the horseman who is supposed to diminish the bull's power by sticking his long lance into the bull's neck. Once this job has been done, the aids attract the bull's attention in order to allow the horseman to withdraw. Now it is the turn of the banderilleros. These men are provided with a pair of small picks which they hold one in each hand. They challenge the bull, inviting him to attack, by moving their arms up and down and by running towards the animal or parallel to it. When the bull finally attacks, they avoid his pass and at the same time stick their banderillas into his back. This is done for three consecutive times with the purpose of increasing the bull's fierceness so that he will be wild and courageous when the matador calls him to die.

Right after the third pair of banderillas, the trumpet sounds again and the second and most important part of the performance begins. This part is called the *lidiando el toro*. The matador sends everybody behind the fence and faces the spectators. He offers the death of the bull to some particular person, usually a lady, changes his big cape for a smaller piece of red cloth and a curved sword, and starts walking towards the bull. Now is when the master must show his mastery and his courage. He lets the bull attack him again and again while he avoids the deadly horns without moving his feet.

After the matador has shown all of his art and skill against the bull's attacks, the trumpet sounds for the last time, and the third part of the performance begins. This is called the *momento de la verdad*, the moment of truth. The master allows the bull a few more passes at him in order to place it in a convenient part of the ring. Then he takes the sword in his right hand, aims at the highest part of the bull's back, lowers his small cape, bends his left knee, and at the same time that the bull moves his head toward the cape, he introduces the curved sword into the bull's spine, hoping to bisect the jugular vein. If the thrust is successful, the bull will die in a few seconds. If the master fails, besides hearing ugly comments from the spectators, he will have to try again and again, until the bull finally dies. Then the bull's corpse will be dragged away by four or six horses. This marks the end of the first performance, to be repeated until the sixth bull dies and the fiesta comes to an end.

Matthew Kay

A Man Who Writes a Poem

A man who writes a poem
floats in space
No one can tell
where the buoyancy comes from

A man who writes a poem
is like a pianist
whose hands are already moving
before the key's been chosen consciously

His hands precede him
His hands caught by the sound cannot escape
which is why they struggle

The sound guides the hands
and the hands
trying to escape the sound
drag him along
somewhere
       Where?

To see the shape
of a man writing a poem
jump off the highest place in the world
upside down

And then your falling eye the wrong way up
might catch a glimpse
of a man writing a poem
floating in space inside the gloom

Tamura Ryûichi

Young, Gifted and Black

*'To be young, gifted and black,
Oh what a lovely precious dream ...'*

I can still hear the bright, lilting voices rising up above the usual hum, shouts and shrieks from the tarmac playground, filtering through large dust-smeared windows of a classroom in north-west London. At least the windows on the first floor weren't decorated with wire-mesh like those at ground level.

Below, the barren grey rectangle which served as the girls' play area was completely hemmed in. Overshadowed on one side by the large Victorian building, it was also bordered by a wire fence separating it from the street, a long dark bicycle shed with the outdoor toilets at one end, and a high wall. All the brickwork, once newly red, had become encrusted with the grime and soot from decades of smoke belched out through surrounding chimneys. Not from the east, however, where - past the fire station, hospital and park - stretched leafy, gardened streets and houses with drives, shrubberies and central heating. No, the culprit chimneys squatted to the north, west and south, above row after row of narrow, tightly packed houses, hugging the factories and the giant industrial complexes which had originally spawned them. The greatest culprits were the factory chimneys themselves - enormous hulks on the sky-line, asserting their dominance even over the air people breathed. Day and night the factories sucked in the parents of the children in the playground.

It was my first year of teaching in a secondary school, having moved from a primary school, and I had actually chosen to come here. The headmaster was a character well-known for his views on equality and opportunity. I can still remember my excitement on seeing the job advertised. 'Teacher required for remedial class. Primary experience an advantage.'

But despite my positive wish to work in this particular school, I wasn't the first person chosen to fill the post. The other two applicants were both offered the job before me and turned it down. In the course of being shown around the school, we had learnt that the class in question had been through two or three teachers the previous year! I remained undeterred, eager to try out my ideas. I imagined an immediate identity with the students. I too was an immigrant, albeit white. Most of those in the 'remedial' class were black, many having come from the Caribbean as young children, leaving the close-knit warmth of grandparents to join parents (whom they hadn't seen for a number of years) in cold, grey Britain. After the freedom of a largely outdoor life, most of them now lived in rented accommodation, sharing limited space and facilities with other families. I too had left behind a land which at least physically was very beautiful. I had come out of the social ugliness and repression of South Africa. Although our circumstances were so different, I felt I understood something of the trauma those children had experienced in being uprooted. I wanted to work with them. Together we could make it.

I should have gleaned more, however, from the interview about the qualities on which I was being judged. My enthusiasm obviously didn't carry a very high rating. It had way exceeded that of the other candidates and yet each had been offered the job first. I remember sitting isolated on a seat well below the level of a podium on which sat the headmaster and two other interviewers, secure behind a large table. Perhaps my memory has exaggerated the gap between us. There must have been a question mark in their minds as to whether I was 'tough' enough not to be the class's next nine-pin. Was I going to be simply another loose link in the school's chain of armour? I couldn't see the problem. To me the fight was to be waged against illiteracy and other evils. My students and I were going to be on the same side. Well, for want of a more reliable candidate, I was employed.

It was on my first day in my new classroom that the head of the lower school entered before the bell rang, for a brief, friendly chat. He was a large, fatherly man and, as I was to find out, not averse to using a fatherly cane.

"Do you know what words you should see inscribed above your door every time you walk through it?" he asked.

"No," I replied, looking at the faded green paint.

"The words are 'REMEMBER YOU ARE THE BOSS'. Remember that and you'll be all right. But come to me if you need any help."

He stayed to introduce me to my class and was gone.

It didn't take me long to realise the way things really were in the school. To my students I was another one of 'them' to their 'us'. To most of the staff, the students were 'them' to our 'us'. The role was ready made and I had stepped into it.

Almost all I can remember of those first months more than seventeen years ago is a sense of struggle. After my naive imaginings had been quickly shattered, I decided not to sink. My priority became to stay afloat. If I could at least stay intact, I would see what I could retrench of my hopes - afterwards.

My mind has the useful facility of throwing a blanket over details of unpleasant memories. Had someone been able to video my classroom behaviour in those early days, I would surely cringe. The two experiences I do clearly remember were to do with my own confrontation with authority. Having discovered that my place was amongst the front-line troops (in a war I didn't want to fight but which was nevertheless in progress) I made two attempts to assert a limited independence.

The first was over my right to wear trousers. It appeared that only the women PE staff wore trousers, but I simply ignored the norm and wore them too. I received some surprised looks and queries, particularly from other women members of staff.

"Hasn't the head said anything to you?"

I waited ... with my plan. It was the time of the mini-skirt and over my trousers I wore tops that were practically 'mini' length. If the headmaster expressed his disapproval, I was going to strip off the trousers and say, "All right! Is this more suitable?"

In fact it never happened. The lower school head called me into his office and told me discreetly that my trousers had come to the attention of the headmaster but he had decided not to pursue the matter!

My second confrontation had a less satisfactory ending. The school had become a comprehensive, combined from an ex-grammar and an ex-secondary modern. Our Victorian building, the lower school, was the old secondary modern, while the upper section used the grammar school building, set well away from us in the leafy, gardened part of the suburb. When it was announced that we were to have a Speech Day with prizes, which I was expected to attend, I was taken aback. None of my students was to receive anything. In the lower school they were already isolated, known in the playground as the 'thickies', the 'dumbos' and such like. All the other classes were 'mixed-ability' except for the 'remedials'. I was doing battle with my students not to accept the label and to upgrade their own expectations. I had already made out that the majority of them were in my class largely for social reasons. They possessed a range of abilities which weren't flourishing and weren't recognised. I had begun to realise that the very way the school was organised - the way they had been isolated into a 'remedial' class - was a major part of their 'problem'. Certainly not lack of intelligence.

So, not deterred by my lowly status, I wrote to the headmaster. It was an honest letter, expressing concern that my students were not involved in the prize-giving. I think I also added that I believed Speech Days were a relic from the grammar school ... and shouldn't we be looking for new ways to reward and celebrate achievements in a comprehensive school? I declined the invitation to attend the ceremony.

I was quite unprepared for the response that followed. I must have naively supposed that although the headmaster mightn't agree, his political outlook should at least allow him to listen. Instead, I received an icy visit from the deputy headmistress - from the Upper School. A rare event down our way! The head was most upset. It wasn't true that my students were ignored. They were simply being cared for in other ways more suited to them. It was a great disappointment to the head that I didn't recognise this. The conversation was not a two-way affair and I didn't attend Speech Day. The following year when the event came round again, I explained that I had a relative from abroad passing briefly through London. That mundane excuse seemed to be more acceptable than my letter of the previous year.

Slowly, as the individual personalities of my students began to emerge, and as we got to know each other better, we began to develop ways of working which I can reflect on now without the sense of shame that shades the other parts. Perhaps it was in reading together and talking about books both they and I enjoyed that we came to share something.

But, just as we all continued to breathe in whatever the surrounding chimneys were emitting, our lives were always overshadowed by bigger issues. Racism was a major one. There were daily examples. Coming from South Africa I had ears and eyes sensitive to the myriad forms of insult and abuse, however slight or casual.

A couple of incidents remain particularly clear. I can still see the intense humiliation and hurt in the eyes of a large sturdy boy, usually well able to look after himself. He had come to school wearing leather sandals and on entering the classroom with a smile, another child had called out.

"Hey you, Zulu!"

Both boys were black and the wearer of the sandals retaliated fiercely, "I'm not!"

Nothing I said at the time about how pleased and proud he could be - of how he could take 'Zulu' as a compliment - seemed able to remove for him the stigma of the words. He insisted in attending assembly in his socks. So racism eats into the soul.

The other event had a happier outcome. One of my students had come from Kenya to stay with an older brother, while his parents had returned to India. The word 'Paki' could be heard from both white and black students. I recall a group of black students coming into class from the playground one day, absolutely jubilant. On their shoulders they carried the Kenyan boy who was grinning broadly.

"Nanji's done it, Miss! He did it!"

"What?" I asked.

"There were these white boys, Miss. They called him 'Paki' and tried to jump him. But he hit them, Miss! He sent them flying!"

A bond had been forged. Nanji had withstood a racist attack by fighting back. He had been through the fire and become one of the boys.

This brings me back to the words of the song with which I began this reminiscence. It was while I was finding myself sucked into a system and a role with which I had little sympathy, that I first heard these wonderfully resistant lyrics, sung with a rhythm and delight that seemed to defy those high walls, the wire fence, the poky, dirty streets and the factory gate at the end of the road. Most of all the lovely voices defied narrow, twisted minds. I hoped the woodwork master was listening. When I went down to the playground there was a group of four black girls, standing by the bicycle shed, oblivious to stares and comments. Their eyes were shining as they kept up their harmonies.

Their singing, and this particular song, became a regular breaktime event for a while. I can't remember exactly when it stopped. It was some time after it had reached number five in the charts with Bob and Marcia. Perhaps it was when one of the four was sent away to a school for 'maladjusted' children. Somehow I felt she would take the song with her.

Beverley Naidoo

We are not a Sub-Species ...

The worst thing about being a teenager is the word 'teenager'. Being a teenager doesn't feel any different to being a normal person. I don't seem to be undergoing any emotional traumas or identity crises - I must be letting somebody down. The word teenager prevents some people from treating adolescents as young adults; in their eyes we are some kind of sub-species.

My sixth form used to be regularly visited by various speakers. One week the local insurance man came. In an unfortunate effort to obtain group participation and yet remain in control of the talk, he treated 200 intelligent 18-year-olds like a load of morons. Smiling benignly he said: "Now, what do we find under roads?" The answers he received - worms, moles and dead insurance men - were not what he was looking for. Actually it was pipelines. Ask a stupid question! The point is, that man would not have spoken to adults in the same way, so why to teenagers? If you treat people like idiots, they act like idiots.

There might not be much difference between a 34-year-old and a 38-year-old, but there's a hell of a lot of difference between a 14-year-old and a 18-year-old. When I was 13, I thought that being in the fifth form was the ultimate in maturity: I could wear a navy jumper instead of the putrid regulation royal blue. Now at the worldly age of 18, 16 seems a mere nothing.

The word teenager is misleading because it leads to generalisations and it is so derogatory. For many adults there is no such thing as a teenager who doesn't like discos - if you happen not to, as many teenagers don't - they label you an awkward, antisocial adolescent. For a short time I was a waitress in a restaurant. The average age of the staff was 19, that of the clientele about 40. We, the staff, used to watch amused and slightly disgusted as overweight middle-aged swingers, who in the light of day would claim that discos were a load of teenage nonsense, jerked violently around to the latest hits - as they say. (They were either dancing or having heart attacks - I couldn't quite tell). If, in the eyes of adults, 'teenage culture' is such a contemptible thing, why, given the opportunity, do they throw themselves into it with so much enthusiasm and a lot less style?

I may be cynical, but I think it's partly due to jealousy. Some adults patronise teenagers because they are envious of their youth and because the respect they don't get from their peers, they demand from their juniors. Even on the lofty level of our local tennis club, this type of jealousy rears its head, or rather, swings its racket. If we were to put forward our strongest women's team, it would consist entirely of teenage girls. Of course, this never happens. The elder women play by virtue of their age, not skill. After all, teenage girls don't count as women.

It always seems like sour grapes to me, when I say something predictable like "I won't get married," and adults smile knowingly and say equally as predictably "You'll soon change". Whether they believe I'll change or not, doesn't matter, what they don't like is that I'm indirectly criticising their way of life. Also, I'm enjoying a freedom of opinion and expression they never had. What their 'You'll soon change' actually means is: 'Shut up you stupid girl, you don't know what you're talking about. We know best.' I don't think you would find such narrow-mindedness in an adolescent.

If there is such a thing as a teenager, it refers to a state of mind and not a particular age range. At 20 you don't automatically become an adult because you dropped the 'teen' in your age. Unfortunately 'teenager' has come to connote things like selfishness, irresponsibility, and arrogance. This means there are a lot of adults around who are still teenage. Equally, if maturity is measured by attributes such as compassion and tolerance, and not merely the number of years you've totted up, then there are a lot of adult teenagers around.

I would like the word 'teenager' to be banned, but I suppose that would never happen, as a lot of people would stop making a lot of money.

Lois McNay

Michael Jackson

Michael Jackson, Megastar. His LP, *Thriller*, made in 1982, has sold over 35 million copies worldwide and is said to be the biggest selling LP in the history of pop. Jackson is reputed to have amassed a personal fortune of some 75 million dollars at the age of 26. Even more remarkably, he's been a star since he was 11 and sang lead with his brothers in the Jackson Five, the biggest selling group on the Tamla Motown label in the 1970s. The Jackson Five practically invented the genre of 'teeny-bopper' pop cashed in upon by white pop idols like Donny Osmond. While such figures have faded from memory, classic Jackson Five tunes like 'I Want You Back' and 'ABC' can still evoke the pride and enthusiasm which marked the assertive mood of the 'Black Pride' cultural movement.

After he and his brothers left Motown in the mid-1970s and took more artistic control over their own productions, Jackson developed as a singer, writer and stage performer. His *Off The Wall* LP of 1979, which established him as a solo star, demonstrates the lithe, sensual texture of his voice and its mastery over a diverse range of musical styles and idioms, from romantic ballad to rock. Just what is it that makes this young, black man so different, so appealing?

Undoubtedly, it is the voice which lies at the heart of his appeal. Rooted in the Afro-American tradition of 'soul', Jackson's vocal performance is characterised by breathy gasps, squeaks, sensual sighs and other wordless sounds which have become his stylistic signature. The way in which this style punctuates the emotional resonance and bodily sensuality of the music corresponds to what Roland Barthes called the 'grain' of the voice - 'the grain is the body in the voice as it sings'. The emotional and erotic expressiveness of the voice is complemented by the sensual grace and sheer excitement of Jackson's dancing style: even as a child, his stage performance provoked comparisons with James Brown and Jackie Wilson.

But there is another element to Jackson's success and popularity - his image. Jackson's individual style fascinates and attracts attention. The ankle-cut jeans, the single-gloved hand and, above all, the wet-look hairstyle which have become his trademarks, have influenced the sartorial repertoires of black and white youth cultures and been incorporated into mainstream fashion.

Most striking is the change in Jackson's looks and physical appearance as he has grown. The cute child dressed in gaudy flower-power gear and sporting a huge 'Afro' hairstyle has become, as a young adult, a paragon of racial and sexual ambiguity. Michael reclines across the gatefold sleeve of the *Thriller* LP, dressed in crisp black and white on a glossy metallic surface against a demure pink background. Look closer - the glossy sheen of his complexion appears lighter in colour than before; the nose seems sharper, more aquiline, less rounded and 'African' and the lips seem tighter, less pronounced. Above all, the large 'Afro' has dissolved into a shock of wet-look permed curls and a new stylistic trademark, the single lock over the forehead, appears.

What makes this reconstruction of Jackson's image more intriguing is the mythology built up around it, in which it is impossible or simply beside the point to distinguish truth from falsehood. It is said that he has undergone cosmetic surgery to adopt a more white, European look, although Jackson denies it. But the definite sense of racial ambiguity writ large in his new image is at the same time, and by the same token, the site of a sexual ambiguity bordering on androgyny. He may sing as sweet as Al Green, dance as hard as James Brown, but he looks more like Diana Ross than any black male soul artist. The media have seized upon these ambiguities and have fabricated a 'persona', a private 'self' behind the image, which has become the subject of speculation and rumour. This mythologisation has culminated in the construction of a Peter Pan figure. We are told that behind the star's image is a lonely, 'lost boy', whose life is shadowed by morbid obsessions and anxieties. He lives like a recluse and is said to 'come alive' only when he is on stage in front of his fans. The media's exploitation of public fascination with Jackson the celebrity has even reached the point of 'pathologising' his personality:

Even Michael Jackson's millions of fans find his lifestyle strange. It's just like one of his hit songs, Off The Wall. People in the know
 say -
His biggest thrill is taking trips to Disneyland.
His closest friends are zoo animals.
He talks to tailor's dummies in his lounge.
He fasts every Sunday and then dances in his bedroom until he drops of exhaustion. So showbusiness folk keep asking the question: "Is Jacko Wacko?"
Two top American psychiatrists have spent hours examining a detailed dossier on Jackson.

Jackson's sexuality and sexual preference in particular have been the focus for such public fascination, as a business associate of his,

Shirley Brooks, complains:

> He doesn't and won't make public statements about his sex life, because he believes - and he is right - that is none of anyone else's business. Michael and I had a long conversation about it, and he felt that anytime you're in the public eye and don't talk to the press, they tend to make up these rumours to fill their pages.

Kobena Mercer

CHANGING

Orang-utan

A

curve air
I swing/fly
I am a nettle
bow bending in wind
faster than wind
thru' trees
ballet dance,
gymnast on ropes
springboard from sky
Catch me if you can
The arms have it
My god,
the sun
arm power
longer than ...?
Could do what?
swing - trees
Behind - day stars - glitter
piebald
mottle
How many toes?
dapple
dappled day
halved-in light
[skewbald?]
light
grip
Christmas tree fairy
on top of magic tree

B

I am...
soundless
-snatch
show off
catch me
watch
touch
trick-of-the-light
breath/fur licks
curved air
Watch me,
touch me,
catch-me-if you can!
leap
I am
soundless
trick-of-the-light
say/sway
dare me
a curve of air a lick of curved air
wide?
bow, bending on trees
fresh from the night
I will push open
push/break?
See me stretch open
this dappled day
with my long arm of the law
I have the world in my grip
I am....
the long arm of
more the law
war?
enter from
the wings
between sky
floor saw
Get a grip on the world

Not everyone is aware of the difficulties in drafting a poem. Judith Nicholls wrote 13 drafts of her poem Orang-utan before she was satisfied with it. Here she explains some of the stages involved.

A (draft 1)

The first important task is to get something down; staring at a blank page waiting for the perfect words is a guarantee for paralysis.

Sometimes teachers are tempted to sift the material, discarding anything they see as 'inappropriate'. At first none of the ideas are 'right' or 'wrong'. Sifting discourages the free-flow of ideas and unusual lines of thought may be lost.

Not all ideas in the draft were used in the final poem, but they provided a useful starting point. The next draft would go on to show the tentative, sketchy beginnings of a poem.

B (draft 4)

See me stretch open ...? See me push wide ...? Making a poem involves constant choice; in order to make those choices the poem must be heard aloud.

Even infants have firm opinions about their preferred word choice and order in their poems. Many children love to rhyme - but do it badly.

Near-rhyme (watch/touch/catch, trick/crack) can usefully extend word-choice and add interesting echoes. Rhyming words can be used anywhere in the poem: together, in the middle of lines or at the beginning, as here.

D

```
Watch me,
touch me,
catch-me-if-you-can!
I am
soundless, ——— groundless?
swung-out-of-sight,
gone with the wind,
track of curved air,
trick-of-the-light.

Watch me,
touch me,
catch-me-if you-dare!
I hide, I glide,
I stride through air,
shatter the day-stars' dapple
over forest floor.
The world's in my grasp!
I am windsong,
sky-flier,
ruler of trees,
the arm of the law.
```

NB. They don't leap - reach, from branch to branch!

Name means man-of-the-woods

—day?

I am windsong,
man of the woods
sky-flier,
man-of-the-woods,
the arm of the law

C

I have the world
the world in my grasp
I'm the arm of the law
my arm is the law

Orang-utan **E**

```
Watch me,
 touch me,
 catch-me-if-you-can!
I am
 soundless,
 swung-from-your-sight,
 gone with the wind,
 shiver of air,
 trick-of-the-light.

Watch me,
 touch me,
 catch-me-if you-dare!
I hide, I glide,
 I stride through air,
 shatter the day-star dappled light
 over forest floor.
The world's in my grasp!
I am windsong,
 sky-flier,
 man-of-the-woods,
 the arm of the law.
```

C (draft 6)

The crafting work continues ... Pupils often write rather 'prosey' poems because they give insufficient thought to where their lines should end. A good reading aloud of various options will clarify where they want line breaks.

D (draft 8)

A poem should explore, excite, bring alive - but it can still be accurate! I abandoned the word 'leap' after further research, but was delighted to discover that orang-utan in the Malay language means 'old man of the woods'.

Scientific or historical research projects can contain exciting background material for later poems.

E (draft 13)

The finished poem. The animal is named in the title only, so that the poem can try to communicate in the minimum number of words some small part of the essence of the creature. Young writers can be encouraged to check for spare words which make for prosiness: every word should work for its keep.

Judith Nicholls

If I Were a Man

"If I were a man ...," that was what pretty little Mollie Mathewson always said when Gerald would not do what she wanted him to - which was seldom.

That was what she said this bright morning, with a stamp of her little high-heeled slipper, just because he had made a fuss about that bill, the long one with the 'account rendered,' which she had forgotten to give him the first time and been afraid to the second - and now he had taken it from the postman himself.

Mollie was 'true to type.' She was a beautiful instance of what is reverentially called 'a true woman.' Little, of course - no true woman may be big. Pretty, of course - no true woman could possibly be plain. Whimsical, capricious, charming, changeable, devoted to pretty clothes and always 'wearing them well,' as the esoteric phrase has it. (This does not refer to the clothes - they do not wear well in the least - but to some special grace of putting them on and carrying them about, granted to but few, it appears.)

She was also a loving wife and a devoted mother possessed of 'the social gift' and the love of 'society' that goes with it, and, with all these was fond and proud of her home and managed it as capably as - well, as most women do.

If ever there was a true woman it was Mollie Mathewson, yet she was wishing heart and soul she was a man.

And all of a sudden she was!

She was Gerald, walking down the path so erect and square-shouldered, in a hurry for his morning train, as usual, and, it must be confessed, in something of a temper.

Her own words were ringing in her ears - not only the 'last word,' but several that had gone before, and she was holding her lips tight shut, not to say something she would be sorry for. But instead of acquiescence in the position taken by that angry little figure on the veranda, what she felt was a sort of superior pride, a sympathy as with weakness, a feeling that 'I must be gentle with her,' in spite of the temper.

A man! Really a man - with only enough subconscious memory of herself remaining to make her recognize the differences.

At first there was a funny sense of size and weight and extra thickness, the feet and hands seemed strangely large, and her long, straight, free legs swung forward at a gait that made her feel as if on stilts.

This presently passed, and in its place, growing all day, wherever she went, came a new and delightful feeling of being *the right size*.

Everything fitted now. Her back snugly against the seat-back, her feet comfortably on the floor. Her feet? . . . His feet! She studied them carefully. Never before, since her early school days, had she felt such freedom and comfort as to feet - they were firm and solid on the ground when she walked; quick, springy, safe - as when, moved by an unrecognizable impulse, she had run after, caught, and swung aboard the car.

Another impulse fished in a convenient pocket for change - instantly, automatically, bringing forth a nickel for the conductor and a penny for the newsboy.

These pockets came as a revelation. Of course she had known they were there, had counted them, made fun of them, mended them, even envied them; but she never had dreamed of how it *felt* to have pockets.

Behind her newspaper she let her consciousness, that odd mingled consciousness, rove from pocket to pocket, realising the armored assurance of having all those things at hand, instantly get-at-able, ready to meet emergencies. The cigar case gave her a warm feeling of comfort - it was full; the firmly held fountain pen, safe unless she stood on her head; the keys, pencils, letters, documents, notebook, checkbook, bill folder - all at once, with a deep rushing sense of power and pride, she felt what she had never felt before in all her life - the possession of money, of her own earned money - hers to give or to withhold, not to beg for, tease for, wheedle for - hers.

That bill - why, if it had come to her - to him, that is - he would have paid it as a matter of course, and never mentioned it - to her.

Then, being he, sitting there so easily and firmly with his money in his pockets, she wakened to his life-long consciousness about money. Boyhood - its desires and dreams, ambitions. Young manhood - working tremendously for the wherewithal to make a home - for her. The present years with all their net of cares and hopes and dangers; the present moment, when he needed every cent for special plans of great importance, and this bill, long overdue and demanding payment, meant an amount of inconvenience wholly unnecessary if it had been given him when it first came; also, the man's keen dislike of that 'account rendered.'

"Women have no business sense!" she found herself saying. "And all that money just for hats - idiotic, useless, ugly things!"

With that she began to see the hats of the women in the car as she had never seen hats before. The men's seemed normal, dignified, becoming, with enough variety for personal taste, and with distinction in style and in age, such as she had never noticed before. But the women's ...

With the eyes of a man and the brain of a man; with the memory of a whole lifetime of free action wherein the hat, close-fitting on cropped hair, had been no handicap; she now perceived the hats of women.

The massed fluffed hair was at once attractive and foolish, and on that hair, at every angle, in all colors, tipped, twisted, tortured into every crooked shape, made of any substance chance might offer, perched these formless objects. Then, on their formlessness the trimmings - these squirts of stiff feathers, these violent outstanding bows of glistening ribbon, these swaying, projecting masses of plumage which tormented the faces of bystanders.

Never in all her life had she imagined that this idolized millinery could look, to those who paid for it, like the decorations of an insane monkey.

And yet, when there came into the car a little woman, as foolish as any, but pretty and sweet-looking, up rose Gerald Mathewson and gave her his seat. And, later, when there came in a handsome red-cheeked girl, whose hat was wilder, more violent in color and eccentric in shape than any other - when she stood nearby and her soft curling plumes swept his cheek once and again - he felt a sense of sudden pleasure at the intimate tickling touch - and she, deep down within, felt such a wave of shame as might well drown a thousand hats forever.

When he took his train, his seat in the smoking car, she had a new surprise. All about him were the other men, commuters too, and many of them friends of his.

To her, they would have been distinguished as 'Mary Wade's husband,' 'the man Belle Grant is engaged to,' 'that rich Mr Shopworth,' or 'that pleasant Mr Beale.' And they would all have lifted their hats to her, bowed, made polite conversation if near enough - especially Mr Beale.

Now came the feeling of open-eyed acquaintance, of knowing men - as they were. The mere amount of this knowledge was a surprise to her - the whole background of talk from boyhood up, the gossip of barber-shop and club, the conversation of morning and evening hours on trains, the knowledge of political affiliation, of business standing and prospects, of character - in a light she had never known before.

They came and talked to Gerald, one and another. He seemed quite popular. And as they talked, with this new memory and new understanding, an understanding which seemed to include all these men's minds, there poured in on the submerged consciousness beneath a new, a startling knowledge - what men really think of women.

Good, average American men were there; married men for the most part, and happy - as happiness goes in general. In the minds of each and all there seemed to be a two-storey department, quite apart from the rest of their ideas, a separate place where they kept their thoughts and feelings about women.

In the upper half were the tenderest emotions, the most exquisite ideals, the sweetest memories, all lovely sentiments as to 'home' and 'mother,' all delicate admiring adjectives, a sort of sanctuary, where a veiled statue, blindly adored, shared place with beloved yet commonplace experiences.

In the lower half - here that buried consciousness woke to keen distress - they kept quite another assortment of ideas. Here, even in this clean-minded husband of hers, was the memory of stories told at men's dinners, of worse ones overheard in street or car, of base traditions, coarse epithets, gross experiences - known, though not shared.

And all these in the department 'woman,' while in the rest of the mind - here was new knowledge indeed.

The world opened before her. Not the world she had been reared in - where Home had covered all the map, almost, and the rest had been 'foreign,' or 'unexplored country,' but the world as it was - man's world, as made, lived in, and seen, by men.

It was dizzying. To see the houses that fled so fast across the car window, in terms of builders' bills, or of some technical insight into materials and methods; to see a passing village with lamentable knowledge of who 'owned it' and of how its Boss was rapidly aspiring in state power, or of how that kind of paving was a failure; to see shops, not as mere exhibitions of desirable objects, but as business ventures, many mere sinking ships, some promising a profitable voyage - this new world bewildered her.

She - as Gerald - had already forgotten about that bill, over which she - as Mollie - was still crying at home. Gerald was 'talking business' with this man, 'talking politics' with that, and now sympathizing with the carefully withheld troubles of a neighbor.

Mollie had always sympathized with the neighbor's wife before.

She began to struggle violently with this large dominant masculine consciousness. She remembered with sudden clearness things she had read, lectures she had heard, and resented with increasing intensity this serene masculine preoccupation with the male point of view.

Mr Miles, the little fussy man who lived on the other side of the street, was talking now. He had a large complacent wife; Mollie had never liked her much, but had always thought him rather nice - he was so punctilious in small courtesies.

And here he was talking to Gerald - such talk!

"Had to come in here," he said. "Gave my seat to a dame who was bound to have it. There's nothing they won't get when they make up their minds to it—eh?"

"No fear!" said the big man in the next seat. "They haven't much mind to make up, you know - and if they do, they'll change it."

"The real danger," began the Rev Alfred Smythe, the new Episcopal clergyman, a thin, nervous, tall man with a face several centuries behind the times, "is that they will overstep the limits of their God-appointed sphere."

"Their natural limits ought to hold 'em, I think," said cheerful Dr Jones. "You can't get around physiology, I tell you."

"I've never seen any limits, myself, not to what they want, anyhow," said Mr Miles. "Merely a rich husband and a fine house and no end of bonnets and dresses, and the latest thing in motors, and a few diamonds - and so on. Keeps us pretty busy."

There was a tired gray man across the aisle. He had a very nice wife, always beautifully dressed, and three unmarried daughters, also beautifully dressed - Mollie knew them. She knew he worked hard, too, and she looked at him now a little anxiously.

But he smiled cheerfully.

"Do you good, Miles," he said. "What else would a man work for? A good woman is about the best thing on earth."

"And a bad one's the worst, that's sure," responded Miles.

"She's a pretty weak sister, viewed professionally," Dr Jones averred with solemnity, and the Rev Alfred Smythe added, "She brought evil into the world."

Gerald Mathewson sat up straight. Something was stirring in him which he did not recognize - yet could not resist.

"Seems to me we all talk like Noah," he suggested drily. "Or the ancient Hindu scriptures. Women have their limitations, but so do we, God knows. Haven't we known girls in school and college just as smart as we were?"

"They cannot play our games," coldly replied the clergyman.

Gerald measured his meager proportions with a practiced eye.

"I never was particularly good at football myself," he modestly admitted, "but I've known women who could outlast a man in all-round endurance. Besides - life isn't spent in athletics!"

This was sadly true. They all looked down the aisle where a heavy ill-dressed man with a bad complexion sat alone. He had held the top of the columns once, with headlines and photographs. Now he earned less than any of them.

"It's time we woke up," pursued Gerald, still inwardly urged to unfamiliar speech. "Women are pretty much *people*, seems to me. I know they dress like fools - but who's to blame for that? We invent all those idiotic hats of theirs, and design their crazy fashions, and, what's more, if a woman is courageous enough to wear common-sense clothes - and shoes - which of us wants to dance with her?

"Yes, we blame them for grafting on us, but are we willing to let our wives work? We are not. It hurts our pride, that's all. We are always criticizing them for making mercenary marriages, but what do we call a girl who marries a chump with no money? Just a poor fool, that's all. And they know it.

"As for Mother Eve - I wasn't there and can't deny the story, but I will say this. If she brought evil into the world, we men have had the lion's share of keeping it going ever since - how about that?"

They drew into the city, and all day long in his business, Gerald was vaguely conscious of new views, strange feelings, and the submerged Mollie learned and learned.

Charlotte Perkins Gilman

© Posy Simmonds 1978

Woman

How sad it is to be framed in woman's form!
Nothing on earth is held so cheap.
A boy that comes to a home
Drops to earth like a god that chooses to be born.
His bold heart braves the Four Oceans,
The wind and dust of a thousand miles.
No one is glad when a girl is born;
By *her* the family sets no store.
When she grows up, she hides in her room
Afraid to look a man in the face.
No one cries when she leaves her home -
Sudden as clouds when the rain stops.
She bows her head and composes her face,
Her teeth are pressed on her red lips.
She bows and kneels countless times,
She must humble herself even to the servants.
While his love lasts he is distant as the stars;
She is a sun-flower, looking up to the sun.
Soon their love will be severed more than water from fire;
A hundred evils will be heaped upon her.
Her face will follow the year's changes;
Her lord will find new pleasures.
They that were once like substance and shadow
Are now as far as Hu and Ch'in.[1]
Yes, Hu and Ch'in shall sooner meet
Than they, whose parting is like Shên and Ch'ên.[2]

Fu Hsüan

[1] The land of the barbarians and China
[2] Evening star and morning star

We're Only Women

We're only women - alas, as it were.
But why alas ? Time to define the reason.
'Wine and women' - so you say.
But we don't talk of 'chocolates and men'!

We distinguish you from buns or toffee
We somehow feel that people are not hams,
Though (to hear you) we only differ
In never having a head upon our shoulders.

'Wine and women'? Let's follow it from there.
Woman, take a cookbook,
Say 'I love you better than jugged hare,
Than strawberry jam! Than pig's feet! Than fish pie!'

Well, how do you like my affection?
You're a person, not a piece of cheese ?
                              - And I?

Novella Matveyeva
(Translated by J.R. Rowland)

Wilfred Owen 1893-1918

'I came out in order to help these boys - directly by leading them as well as an officer can; indirectly, by watching their sufferings that I may speak of them as well as a pleader can. I have done the first.'

October 1918

Wilfred Edward Salter Owen was born in Oswestry on 18 March 1893. His parents were then living in a spacious and comfortable house owned by his grandfather, Edward Shaw. At his death two years later, this former mayor of the city was found to be almost bankrupt, and Tom Owen was obliged to move with his wife and son to lodgings in the backstreets of Birkenhead. They carried with them vivid memories of their vanished prosperity, and Susan Owen resolved that her adored son Wilfred should in time restore the family to its rightful gentility. She was a devout lady, and under her strong influence, Wilfred grew into a serious and slightly priggish boy. At school in Birkenhead and later in Shrewsbury - where Tom Owen was appointed Assistant Superintendent of the Joint Railways in 1906 - he worked hard and successfully, especially at literature and botany. He had begun writing poems when he was 10 or 11, and soon fell under the spell of Keats, who was to remain the principal influence on his work.

Leaving school in 1911, Owen took up a post as lay assistant to the vicar of Dunsden in Oxfordshire. He was to help the vicar with his parish work and receive in return coaching for the university entrance examination that he hoped in due course to sit. Removed from his mother's influence, he became less enamoured of evangelical religion and more critical of the role of the Church - as represented by the vicar of Dunsden - in society. His letters and poems of this period show an increasing awareness of the sufferings of the poor and the first stirrings of the compassion that was to characterize his later poems about the Western Front. He attended botany classes at Reading University and was encouraged by the professor of English to read and write more poetry. In February 1913, on the verge of a nervous breakdown, he left Dunsden and, when he had recovered, crossed to France where he taught at the Berlitz School of Languages in Bordeaux.

He was in the Pyrenees, acting as tutor in a cultivated French household, when war was declared. A visit to a hospital for the

wounded soon opened his eyes to the true nature of war, but it was
not until September 1915 that he finally decided to return to England
and enlist. For several months, he and Edward Thomas were
privates, training at Hare Hall Camp in Essex, but there is no
evidence that they ever met. Commissioned into the Manchester
Regiment, Owen crossed the Channel on 30 December 1916 and, in
the first days of January, joined the 2nd Manchesters on the Somme
near Beaumont Hamel. His letters to his mother tell their own story:

> I have not been at the front.
> I have been in front of it.
> I held an advanced post, that is, a 'dug-out' in the middle of No
> Man's Land.
> We had a march of 3 miles over shelled road then nearly 3
> along a flooded trench. After that we came to where the trenches
> had been blown flat out and had to go over the top. It was of
> course dark, too dark, and the ground was not mud, not sloppy
> mud, but an octopus of sucking clay, 3, 4, and 5 feet deep,
> relieved only by craters full of water. Men have been known to
> drown in them. Many stuck in the mud and only got on by
> leaving their waders, equipment, and in some cases their clothes.
> High explosives were dropping all around us, and machine
> guns spluttered every few minutes. But it was so dark that even
> the German flares did not reveal us.
> Three quarters dead, I mean each of us three quarters dead, we
> reached the dug-out, and relieved the wretches therein. I then
> had to go forth and find another dug-out for a still more
> advanced post where I left 18 bombers. I was responsible for
> other posts on the left but there was a junior officer in charge.
> My dug-out held 25 men tight packed. Water filled it to a depth
> of 1 or 2 feet, leaving say 4 feet of air.
> One entrance had been blown in and blocked.
> So far, the other remained.
> The Germans knew we were staying there and decided we
> shouldn't.
> Those fifty hours were the agony of my happy life.
> Every ten minutes on Sunday afternoon seemed an hour.
> I nearly broke down and let myself drown in the water that
> was now slowly rising over my knees.
> Towards 6 o'clock, when, I suppose, you would be going to
> church, the shelling grew less intense and less accurate: so that I
> was mercifully helped to do my duty and crawl, wade, climb and
> flounder over No Man's Land to visit my other post. It took me
> half an hour to move about 150 yards.
> I was chiefly annoyed by our own machine guns from behind.
> The seeng-seeng-seeng of the bullets reminded me of Mary's
> canary. On the whole I can support the canary better.
> In the Platoon on my left the sentries over the dug-out were

blown to nothing. One of these poor fellows was my first servant whom I rejected. If I had kept him he would have lived, for servants don't do Sentry Duty. I kept my own sentries halfway down the stairs during the more terrific bombardment. In spite of this one lad was blown down and, I am afraid, blinded.

That last experience was to find its way into Owen's poem 'The Sentry', more than a year and a half later.

In March 1917 he fell into a cellar and suffered concussion, and some weeks later, after fierce fighting near St Quentin, was invalided home with shell-shock. At Craiglockhart War Hospital on the outskirts of Edinburgh, he met Siegfried Sassoon, whose first 'war poems' had just appeared in *The Old Huntsman and Other Poems*. Under their influence and with the encouragement and guidance of the older poet, Owen was soon producing poems far superior to any he had written previously. Sassoon not only helped him to purge his style of its early excessive luxuriance, but introduced him to such other poets and novelists as Robert Graves, Arnold Bennett, H. G. Wells and Osbert Sitwell.

It was probably in August 1917 that Owen read the anonymous 'Prefatory Note' to the anthology, *Poems of Today (1916)*, which began:

This book has been compiled in order that boys and girls, already perhaps familiar with the great classics of the English speech, may also know something of the newer poetry of their own day. Most of the writers are living, and the rest are still vivid memories among us, while one of the youngest, almost as these words are written, has gone singing to lay down his life for his country's cause ... there is no arbitrary isolation of one theme from another; they mingle and interpenetrate throughout, to the music of Pan's flute, and of Love's viol, and the bugle-call of Endeavour, and the passing bell of Death.

It is not difficult to imagine him, stung by those sentiments, sitting down to write his 'Anthem for Doomed Youth':

What passing-bells for these who die as cattle?
Only the monstrous anger of the guns.
Only the stuttering rifles' rapid rattle
Can patter out their hasty orisons.
No mockeries now for them; no prayers nor bells;
Nor any voice of mourning save the choirs, -
The shrill, demented choirs of wailing shells;
And bugles calling for them from sad shires.

What candles may be held to speed them all?
Not in the hands of boys but in their eyes
Shall shine the holy glimmers of goodbyes.
The pallor of girls' brows shall be their pall;

Their flowers the tenderness of patient minds,
And each slow dusk a drawing-down of blinds.

Those who die as cattle in a slaughterhouse die in such numbers that there is no time to give them the trappings of a Christian funeral that Owen remembers from his Dunsden days. Instead, they receive a brutal parody of such a service: 'the stuttering rifles' praying (presumably) that they will kill them; the 'choirs ... of shells' wailing as they hunt them down. The bugles may sound the 'Last Post' for them, but they had previously called them to the colours in those same 'sad shires'. So, bitterly but obliquely, Owen assigns to Church and State responsibility for their deaths.

The turn at the end of the octave brings us home, across the Channel, and the sestet opens with a question paralleling the first: 'What candles may be held to speed them all?' It is a gentler question than 'What passing-bells for these who die as cattle?', preparing for the gentler answer that, instead of the parodic rituals offered by rifle, shell and bugle, those who love the soldiers will mark their death with observances more heart-felt, more permanent, than those prescribed by convention:

The pallor of girls' brows shall be their pall;
Their flowers the tenderness of patient minds,
And each slow dusk a drawing-down of blinds.

Many of Owen's other poems spring from a similarly indignant response to a prior text. They, too, are protest poems, directed against many of the same targets as Sassoon's - notably the *old* men of the Army, Church and Government who send *young* men to their death - but, as imaginative and musical structures, they are more complex and reverberant than Sassoon's. Owen's poems also have an important relation to the pastoral tradition of English poetry.

Discharged from Craiglockhart in October, Owen was posted to the 5th Manchesters in Scarborough and there wrote 'The Show' and probably 'Exposure' and 'Strange Meeting'. In March 1918, he was transferred to Ripon. 'The Send-Off', written during this period, is typical of his later work in the way it makes its bitter statement with brilliant economy, its calm surface mined with ironies:

Down the close darkening lanes they sang their way
To the siding-shed,
And lined the train with faces grimly gay.

Their breasts were stuck all white with wreath and spray
As men's are, dead.

Dull porters watched them, and a casual tramp
Stood staring hard,
Sorry to miss them from the upland camp.

Then, unmoved, signals nodded, and a lamp
Winked to the guard.

So secretly, like wrongs hushed-up, they went.
They were not ours:
We never heard to which front these were sent.

Nor there if they yet mock what women meant
Who gave them flowers.

Shall they return to beatings of great bells
In wild train-loads?
A few, a few, too few for drums and yells,

May creep back, silent, to still village wells
Up half-known roads.

At the end of August, Owen was certified 'fit to proceed overseas' and, a month later, was again in action. He was awarded the Military Cross for his part in a successful attack on the Beaurevoir-Fonsomme Line and, before sunrise on the morning of 4 November, led his platoon to the west bank of the Sambre and Oise Canal. They came under murderous fire from German machine guns behind the parapet of the east bank, and at the height of the ensuing battle, Owen was hit and killed while helping his men bring up duck-boards at the water's edge.

In Shrewsbury, the Armistice bells were ringing when his parents' front-door bell sounded its small chime, heralding the telegram they had dreaded for two years.

Jon Stallworthy

Voices and Images of the Great War

Our company had been forward in the attack which gained the plateau and was now called into reserve. We went underground into large caves a little distance in rear of the line. At the mouth of one cave the medical officer was busy attending to the wounded. Those he found to be dead he ordered to be taken out into the open.

We had hardly entered the caves when the Germans counterattacked and we were at once ordered to stand up and fall in ready to go. The sound of the battle heard from the caves was awe-inspiring. Clouds of smoke from bursting shells obscured the dim light which filtered through the cave mouth. Heavy shells crumped into the earth roof of our shelter and machine-guns rat-tat-tatted. The indistinct figures of stretcher-bearers collecting dead and wounded moved in the cloudy light of the cave mouth. We felt trapped and wished ourselves outside fighting instead of standing restless in the semi-darkness. We got nervy and fidgeted and avoided each other's eyes. One soldier at the cave mouth morbidly occupied himself by passing in the names of the latest dead and wounded. I did not want to hear them. Each fresh name bludgeoned my brain with a sense of misery and loss as the litany of familiar names continued and I moved over to my brother's platoon to be near him.

The German attack ceased. It had been beaten back, but the casualties seemed to be very numerous. Outside we saw some of our dead lying in grotesque positions. A few of these had previously cut their long trousers into shorts during the hot August weather, and now they looked like slain schoolboys. A hollow in the ground about ten yards from the caves was filled with bandaged wounded. I was looking at them, envying those with slight wounds who would go away back to England, or, with luck, to Ireland when there was a rising, tearing noise, nearer and nearer, then a shattering burst right on top of us. After a pause and a deep breath I raised my head and saw that the shell had exploded precisely over the hollow and killed every one of the wounded.

Corporal John Lucy
2nd Battalion, Princess Victoria's (Royal Irish Fusiliers) 1914

On Christmas Eve there was a lull in the fighting, no firing going on all after 6 p.m. The Germans had a Christmas tree in the trenches, and Chinese lanterns all along the top of a parapet. Eventually the Germans started shouting, "Come over, I want to speak to you". Our chaps hardly knew how to take this, but one of the 'nuts' belonging to the regiment got out of the trench and started to walk towards the German lines. One of the Germans met him about half-way across, and they shook hands and became quite friendly. In due time the 'nut' came back and told all the others about it. So more of them took it in turns to go and visit the Germans. The officer commanding would not allow more than three men at a time.

I went out myself on Christmas Day and exchanged some cigarettes for cigars, and this game has been going on from Christmas Eve till midnight on Boxing Day without a single round being fired. The German I met had been a waiter in London and could use our language a little. He says they didn't want to fight and I think he was telling the truth as we are not getting half so many bullets as usual. I know this statement will take a bit of believing but it is absolutely correct. Fancy a German shaking your flapper as though he were trying to smash your fingers, and then a few days later trying to plug you. I hardly know what to think about it, but I fancy they are working up a big scheme so that they can give us a doing, but our chaps are prepared, and I am under the impression they will get more than they bargained for.

Gunner Herbert Smith
5th Battery, Royal Field Artillery 1914

The brutality and inhumanity of war stood in great contrast to what I had heard and read about as a youth. I really wanted to go off to the Front at the beginning of the war because in school we were taught to be super patriots. This was drilled into us - in order to be men we should go off to war and, if necessary, bravely die for Kaiser and Fatherland.

When I had joined the army in the spring of 1916 I still carried presumptions that the war would be fought like the 1870 War between Germany and France. Man-to-man combat, for instance. But in the trenches friend and foe alike suffered from the effects of invisible machinery. It was not enough to conquer the enemy. He had to be totally destroyed. The fighting troops of the front lines saw themselves mired hopelessly in this hellish wasteland. Whoever lived through it thanked his good luck. The rest died as 'heroes'. It seemed quite unlikely to me in late 1916 that I should live through it. When you met someone you knew who belonged to a different outfit, he was greeted with the words, "Well, are you still alive?" It was said humorously but meant in deadly earnest. For a young man who had a long and worthwhile future awaiting him, it was not easy to expect death almost daily. However, after a while I got used to the idea of dying young. Strangely, it had a sort of soothing effect and prevented me from worrying too much. Because of this I gradually lost the terrible fear of being wounded or killed.

Freiwilliger Reinhold Spengler
1st Bavarian Infanterie Regiment 1916

You were between the devil and the deep blue sea. If you go forward, you'll likely be shot, if you go back you'll be court-martialled and shot, so what the hell do you do? What can you do? You just go forward because that's the only bloke you can take your knife in, that's the bloke you're facing.

We were sent in to High Wood in broad daylight in the face of heavy machine-gun fire and shell fire, and everywhere there was dead bodies all over the place where previous battalions and regiments had taken part in their previous attacks. We went in there and C Company got a terrible bashing there. It was criminal to send men in broad daylight, into machine gun fire, without any cover of any sort whatsoever. There was no need for it; they could have hung on and made an attack on the flanks somewhere or other, but we had to carry out our orders.

But there was one particular place just before we got to High Wood which was a crossroads, and it was really hell there, they shelled it like anything, you couldn't get past it, it was almost impossible. There were men everywhere, heaps of men, not one or two men, but heaps of men everywhere, all dead. Then afterwards, when our battle was all over, after our attack on High Wood, there was other battalions went up and they got the same! They went on and on. They just seemed to be pushing men in to be killed and no reason. There didn't seem to be any reason. They couldn't possibly take the position, not on a frontal attack. Not at High Wood.

Most of the chaps, actually, they were afraid to go in because they knew it was death. Before we went in, we knew what would happen, some of the blokes that had survived from previous attacks knew what they'd been through. It was hell, it was impossible, utterly impossible. The only possible way to take High Wood was if the Germans ran short of ammunition, they might be able to take it then. They couldn't take it against machine-guns, just ridiculous. It was absolute slaughter. We always blamed the people up above. We had a saying in the Army, 'The higher, the fewer'. They meant the higher the rank, the fewer the brains.

Private W. Hay
The Royal Scots, 1st/9th battalion 1916

O Jesus make it stop

... I am making this statement as an act of wilful defiance of military authority, because I believe that the war is being deliberately prolonged by those who have the power to end it. I am a soldier, convinced that I am acting on behalf of soldiers. I believe that this war, upon which I entered as a war of defence and liberation, has now become a war of aggression and conquest. I believe that the purposes for which I and my fellow soldiers entered upon this war should have been so clearly stated as to have made it impossible to change them, and that, had this been done, the objects which actuated us would now be attainable by negotiation. I have seen and endured the sufferings of the troops, and I can no longer be a party to prolong these sufferings for ends which I believe to be evil and unjust. I am not protesting against the conduct of the war, but against the political errors and insincerities for which the fighting men are being sacrificed. On behalf of those who are suffering now I make this protest against the deception which is being practised on them: also I believe that I may help to destroy the callous complacency with which the majority of those at home regard the continuance of agonies which they do not share, and which they have not sufficient imagination to realise.

Captain Siegfried Sassoon, MC
2nd Battalion, Royal Welch Fusiliers
(As published in *The Times*, 30 July 1917)

Quite suddenly news came that our father was coming home on leave at last. The whole household was jubilant, but there was hardly any food by then (not the kind of food that he would expect and deserve) and very little money.

I remember my mother taking us with her to the shops and standing in a queue for over an hour to get a little extra butter and some cheese on the black market for his supper. We shared her triumph as she came home with a parcel of roasting beef for Father's first dinner. She was so happy that she took us both to meet him off the late troop train from Dover.

I shall never forget Victoria Station with its huge domed glass roof, and the noise of the trains grunting and creaking, and Mother holding tight to our hands in case we were swept away by one of the heavy trolleys which were loaded up with soldiers' bags and haversacks. One of them bumped into a soldier and a girl who were holding each other tightly. The girl was crying and there were tears on the soldier's face too. Mother dragged us away quite crossly. "Don't stare at people when they are sad," she said.

Then the great train came steaming into the station, and suddenly my father was there. He had always seemed to me to be one of the cleanest people in the world; if we hugged him he used to say "Don't touch my collar!" in case our hands were grubby. But there was no need now for this warning. His khaki uniform was crushed and crumpled and there was mud dried on his sleeve. But we all stood and hugged there on Victoria Station. We were all so happy. Someone found a taxi and we bundled in with the huge battered haversack Father had brought with him.

Our cook had dinner all ready, laid out on the dining-room table, delicious roast beef and Yorkshire pudding which she'd made with two of our weekly rationed eggs. Father kept saying, "Goodness! I had no idea you could still eat as well as this in England." We sat up late that night to welcome him home and just as we were going up to bed there was the sound of a whistle in the street and a voice shouting, "Take Cover. Take cover." My sister started to run upstairs to fetch the Ludo and Snakes and Ladders to take down to the basement. Suddenly Father got red and angry and hurried us downstairs. He said in a funny voice, "No time now! You can get them tomorrow!" and I remember his shouting crossly to Rose to see who was peeping between the curtains of the landing window to see if the searchlights had found a zeppelin. He even shouted quite crossly to Mother who waited just a moment behind us to put the fireguard in front of the grate.

We couldn't understand a brave man spoiling all the fun like that.

Anita Mostyn
Daughter of Col Rowland Feilding 1918

Yesterday I visited the battlefield of last year. The place was scarcely recognisable. Instead of a wilderness of ground torn up by shell, a perfect desolation of earth without a sign of vegetation, the ground was a garden of wild flowers and tall grasses. Nature had certainly hidden the ghastly scene under a veil of many colours. I was specially struck by a cross to an unknown British warrior which stood up like a sentinel over the vast cemetery of the fallen in last year's battle, now hidden under the dense vegetation. Most remarkable of all was the appearance of many thousands of white butterflies which fluttered round this solitary grave. You can have no conception of the strange sensation that this host of little fluttering creatures gave me. It was as if the souls of the dead soldiers had come to haunt the spot where so many fell. It was so eerie to see them, the only living things in that wilderness of flowers. And the silence! Not a sound, not even the rustling of a breeze through the grass. It was so still that it seemed as if one could almost hear the beat of the butterflies' wings. Indeed, there was nothing to disturb the eternal slumber of this unknown who was sleeping his last sleep where he fell. A contrast indeed to the hideous crash of battle of a short year ago.

From a British officer at the Front 1919

ACTIVITIES

Being

All the pieces in this section are concerned with being an individual. They each look at different aspects of the self. How do you define yourself, how can you explain your relationship to your family, colour and country?

Only a very few people actually write their own life story and publish an official autobiography but in some ways we are all engaged on our own life story all the time. We chat to family and friends, write letters and diaries, compile photographs in albums: all these are materials for a possible autobiography. Our families and friends build up stories about us, they tell other people about what we get up to now or what we did when we were small; these stories become a part of our own story even when we cannot remember what really happened!

Most people underestimate how interesting they are; they think that the life they lead is somehow duller than everyone else's. For that reason they keep their special and unique view of life locked up inside. Every individual has an incomparable life story. You might consider how that story and the interest that it undoubtedly contains can be used to stimulate and inspire others. What aspects of your life story would make good reading?

It is partly because we each have an individual life story that we are interested in other people's stories too. We know that we can experience some parts of life only through the stories and descriptions of others. We also know that some people are particularly gifted in understanding and explaining their own lives or the lives of the fictional characters they have created. The material in this section will provide you with some insights into other people's lives and, perhaps, help you to make sense of your own.

A final point about making sense of life is that we all have too much experience to deal with. We tend to select certain events, certain moments, and they become very powerful in the mind. The memory stores these significant episodes away until we need to explain them to someone else or, somehow, they pop into our minds uninvited. The material here contains examples of those significant moments and we hope that it will help you to think about the important events from your own life.

Self-portrait
Van Gogh

- Working as a group discuss what you know about the artist. Jot down any details of his life and works you feel sure are accurate and also make a note of any other, less certain, information.
- Look at the picture and write down any ideas or feelings you have about it. Does it add up to what you already knew about the artist or does it change your opinion?
- Working on your own describe what you actually see in this picture. Be detailed and precise and try to comment on his face, his clothes and

so on. Then write down what you feel this picture is actually about. How did Van Gogh feel about himself? Why did he paint this image? Compare your ideas with at least one other person.
● You may prefer to do this piece of work on your own or with someone else. If an artist was commissioned to paint your portrait and asked you how you wished to be painted what would you say? You could begin by thinking about where you might be - would you be sitting or standing? Would you like to show your whole body or just your head and shoulders? Would you want to have any important other people or objects in the picture? What would your expression be in order to reveal your true self? You might find it interesting to compare with others how they imagine themselves in their portraits.

Mirror
Sylvia Plath

Sylvia Plath was a brilliant poet who found it hard to live with her talent. She committed suicide in 1963 at the age of thirty. She left a substantial body of work which has become widely known and closely studied.

● Work with a partner to sum up together what the mirror 'sees'. Is this poem about any mirror or is it the story of a particular mirror in one place? Do you think the mirror has any feelings towards the woman in the poem?
● How well do you know your own face? Do you know someone who would honestly and fairly tell you how you look? Try this as an experiment at home. Look closely at your face in the mirror and note down what you see, then ask someone in your class to read your description and to consider its accuracy. You could also take a photograph of yourself, one that you feel really looks like you, and ask others if they agree.

I'm
Takano Kikuo

The poet comes from Sado Island in the Japanese Sea. He works as an English teacher in Tokyo.

● What kind of person is the writer? He provides us with a description of himself based on contrasting aspects of the same image; what do we learn from this?
● Try writing your own piece based on Kikuo's poem. Do you have two sides or aspects to yourself, depending on what situation you are in?
● Are there several versions of you? How do other people see you? Do they tell you what they think of you? Write a piece about what you hope you are like and how other people may see you or interpret your actions.

A Near Miss
(editors' title)
Ian McEwan

In this extract Stephen is on a journey in a hired car when he finds himself suddenly in a very dangerous situation. One of the main themes in the novel itself is time and the way we are aware of its passing; sometimes it seems to rush by, at other times it goes very slowly indeed.

● Stephen wishes that there had been a witness who reported exactly what happened. Imagine you are that witness and now you are asked to report in court what you saw. Using this passage, work out exactly what occurred and *using only your own words* describe the events. Make sure that you explain what caused the accident as well as the sequence of events.

● In some ways this is a very strange piece of writing - the strangeness comes from the 'slowing of time'. Does McEwan make you feel the slowness as you read? Work with a partner and prepare a reading of this extract, either to perform to someone else or to record on tape. How can your voice (or voices) create a sense of this strange experience?

● Have you ever had an experience similar to Stephen's where time seemed to slow down? Or perhaps you have a memory of a particular event that is absolutely clear in your mind? Try to describe something from your own experience which has the detail and precision of the extract. Write it as a draft and ask others to read it before you write it up finally.

● We are used to slow motion in films and on television. It helps us to see things that the natural eye may miss. With certain kinds of film we can observe how a flower grows or how a humming bird's wing beats. We can also watch an event many times if we replay the film. Can you use your own powers of observation and imagination to create a slow motion sequence in writing? You might describe something dramatic such as an accident or a fire, but equally it might be the fall of a raindrop or the movement of an animal.

---

my father is a retired magician
Ntozake Shange

Ntozake Shange is a playwright and poet whose work is particularly concerned with the lives of black American women.

● The first thing to do with this poem is to work with others on how best to read it aloud. What kind of mood does the poem have? Does it need to be read with an American accent? Would it be best read by several people? Try reading the poem as you think best until you are agreed that you have a good version.

● Is this a jokey or a serious poem?

● The poet uses a distinctive language in the poem, not something called 'standard' English. Try writing out a part of the poem in Standard English and thinking about the difference it makes. Try reading the two versions aloud to see how they sound.

● As well as using a special language, Ntozake Shange makes the poem look unusual on the page. What does she do to achieve this effect? If you have a poem that you would like to write, perhaps about your own background, then why not try writing it in this or a similar way?

● The writer is concerned with her background and her family and she explains that much of her 'irregular behavior' comes from her father. What has influenced you and your behaviour? Can you trace any of your 'odd' habits to other people?

Tokyo Pastoral
Angela Carter

Angela Carter was born in 1940. She is an amazingly varied and productive contemporary writer. She has written novels, short stories and essays and has been involved in other projects such as films, notably *A Company of Wolves*. The following piece describes a time when she was living in Japan, and shows what an acute observer Carter is.

● With a partner work out a new title for the piece - imagine that you are magazine editors and you want to give the essay a 'catchy' title. You also have to select a photograph to illustrate the story. Your job is to choose something from the essay, then a local photographer will go along and take suitable pictures. You have space for up to three pictures. Decide where they would go in the text, and what captions they might have.
● Work with a partner and jot down together what you learn about Tokyo from the essay. Write a brief report to read out to the class.
● Think about somewhere you have visited and write your own descriptive piece, giving your feelings about and impressions of the place.

Theme for English B
Langston Hughes

Langston Hughes was a black American poet, novelist and playwright whose work has been enormously influential. His first collection of poetry was published in 1926 and his last in the year he died, 1967, so that his work spans a period of critical importance for the black American population in terms of civil rights and racial equality.

● What reaction do you think the writer's teacher might have had to this page of 'homework'? Do you think a comment was written at the end of the page?
● Work with a partner and discuss the last few lines of the poem. What kind of relationship is the poet trying to describe?
● Hughes comments that his teacher is 'somewhat more free' than he is. Do you think that the teacher would agree?
● Write a page about yourself. Look closely at the way the poem is written, perhaps discussing the structure with someone else and then write your own piece using that structure.

The Autobiography of Malcolm X
Malcolm X

Malcolm X was one of the most famous radical black leaders of this century. His upbringing in America led him to believe that the best hope for black Americans was to leave the USA and to 'return' to Africa. His life and his views were always extremely controversial and his death by assassination on 4 February 1964 proved how dangerous a life he had led.

● Work in a small group to prepare and record two radio station news reports about the fire in Lansing. Make the reports contrasting in the way that they handle the news.
● Write a letter to Marcus Garvey as if you were Malcolm X's father, explaining what has happened to you and how you feel about

these events.
● Work in a pair and write one or two paragraphs of an encyclopedia-style biographical entry about Malcolm X, using the information from the passage. Think carefully about the kind of language used in encyclopedias. How would the style contrast with autobiographical writing? Compare your paragraphs with the work of another pair.

Seeing

Most of our lives are dominated by other people; family, friends, enemies, politicians, actors, royalty ... . We are all fascinated by others. How well can we ever know anyone else? What makes other people tick? Are other people the same as we are; do they think about the same things as we do? How do you describe other people? Whether you are trying to write a story in which everything is 'made up' or a piece of biography in which every detail is supposed to be real, the problem is the same - what is true? How can you make the reader feel that what you write has the degree of authenticity which makes it worth reading? There are many ways of investigating what is true about others. You can, for example, ask someone about their life. You can set up an interview which will certainly reveal some truth. On the other hand you might rely solely on your imagination, to let your mind create a different kind of truth as important and real as any actual experience.

This section is devoted to ways of seeing, ways of looking at the people who make life worth living. It offers a whole range of writing that can be enjoyed for itself but which also provides models and examples that you might copy or adapt. When describing others, this section shows how much depends on the way that you describe, how important it is to pick out certain details; details which allow the reader to build up a clear picture of what you have in mind.

In looking at others the writers are led on to consider and describe other important ideas and issues. They are never simply describing people, each writer has much more to communicate than merely the details of appearance. Appearance itself may only be the starting point for something much more profound, but becoming a skilled observer of details must be the starting point for anyone who wants to describe people.

By studying how writers create a sense of others we are better able to do the same ourselves. We are also better able to see the different ways in which we can describe what we see.

A great deal of writing about others is designed to make us laugh at what we see. Sometimes this is just for amusement, at other times it it to make us think, too. The material here should help you to consider the way in which humour can be used both to entertain and to raise serious and challenging ideas. It should also help you

to reflect on the fact that serious subjects can be considered in ways that are also amusing. This section may help you to reflect on the important point that real seeing requires a very active kind of looking; the more you look the more you see, and the more interesting and challenging your writing becomes.

Resemblances
Elizabeth Jennings

Elizabeth Jennings was born in Lincolnshire in 1926. She is one of the more influential British poets of the twentieth century. You will find many of her poems in school poetry collections.

● Before reading the poem discuss with a partner whether you think people generally are obsessed with likenesses. When a baby arrives there will always be someone who says, "He/she looks just like his/her dad"! Does it matter whether an individual looks like other members of his or her family? What about people who, for whatever reason, have no close family? Do they come to resemble the people they live with in any way?
● The poem appears to be simple, but can it be immediately understood? Try building up your understanding in stages. Read it to yourself and then jot down your first impressions - you might then read it aloud or listen to someone else's reading. Now add to your impressions - go over the poem again and note any new ideas. At this point work with others in a small group and pool your ideas. What is your collective interpretation of the poem?
● What are your own resemblances? Do you physically resemble some members of your family or have you similar characteristics in any way? Try writing a description of yourself in relation to your parents or other family members.

My Daughter Smokes
Alice Walker

Alice Walker is an American writer, famous for her novel *The Color Purple*. The book has also been used as the basis for a Hollywood film of the same name. As a black woman she writes often about the history of black people in America and about slavery and its legacy of racism. This essay manages to combine some comments on her major themes with a subject that may be very relevant to you.

● Work with a partner and look closely at this piece of writing. Start by jotting down in as few words as possible the argument that Alice Walker wants us to understand. Is there a single message or are there several? What does she want us to consider? For example, is she persuading us with arguments; does she offer evidence as well as personal opinion and experience; is she telling us a story? Once you have thought about these various points try to define this piece of writing, e.g. is it an essay, a description of her family, a story? You may wish to use several terms in your definition.
● Imagine that you are Alice Walker's daughter and that is now three months later. You have decided to give up smoking. Write a letter to

your mother, explaining your decision.
● Work with a small group whose members are interested in the topic of smoking (for whatever reason) and consider the points raised in the article. Alice Walker suggests that there are strong pressures on certain kinds of people to take up smoking. Do you think that is why people, especially teenagers, start the habit? We also know now that inhaling other people's smoke can be harmful; is there an argument for banning smoking in all public places?
● This article contains a number of points which are anti-smoking. What do you think is the best way to deal with this topic? Write a description, story or essay on this topic which you feel could influence its readership.

Sir Thomas More
John Aubrey

John Aubrey lived from 1626 -1697. He was educated at a grammar school and later he trained as a lawyer. At one time Aubrey owned extensive lands and was very wealthy, but he lost almost everything through legal difficulties. This piece comes from his *Brief Lives* which is a collection of short descriptions of important people whom he either knew or was told about. He mixes fact with anecdotes, jokes and rumours, and each of his 'lives' has a real sense of life in it. You will not find his points about Thomas More in many history books.

● Choose someone famous from Aubrey's lifetime or close to it, and find out some established facts about him or her. Once you have these, try writing an Aubrey-style description of that person, making up and adding some odd and amusing extra stories.
● Select a famous living person and describe him or her as Aubrey might have done; this could be especially effective if you use language like Aubrey's.
● Famous people often complain that they have no private lives, that the press in particular are always hounding them. Work in a group and consider whether you think that famous people should accept the fact that the public will always want to know about them.

The Butcher
Craig Raine

The Lavatory Attendant
Wendy Cope

Both these poems are very precise in their descriptions, and although they are about different people they are linked. Consider them together. Craig Raine and Wendy Cope are contemporary poets and both are widely admired for their wit and humour.

● Work in small groups and spend some time on each poem looking at its meaning. What does each writer tell us about the subject of the poem?
● Look very closely at the language of the two poems. How do both writers describe details? How do they make us look again at what might otherwise seem a very familiar and possibly boring detail? How similar are these poems?
● Wendy Cope's poem is to some extent an imitation of Craig Raine's. He has written a number of poems where he uses language in this

special way. Work with someone else and consider these points. Is Wendy Cope's poem a good imitation of Craig Raine's style? Could it be called a parody? Read the two poems again to see whether you feel Wendy Cope's poem is a successful parody.

● Try taking a subject and describing it in the way these two poems do. In other words think carefully what the subject (or object) is like in ordinary language and then find unusual and surprising comparisons to make the reader look again at the subject matter.

● Writing a parody is a challenging exercise and it can be done for many reasons; most writers hope to make us laugh at the original piece that they are parodying. Is there a style of writing that you could parody or 'send up' in some way e.g. a particular newspaper, a politician's speech, science fiction, fantasy, detective, horror, romantic and so on? If you take on this challenge be prepared to spend some time reading an original piece before trying your version.

Observing

This section focusses on the physical world in which we live: places and objects are the dominant subjects. For most of the time we tend not to notice our surroundings nor to pay attention to the objects that surround us; they are simply there. When we encounter something unusual we are struck by it, we notice it and then remember what we observed.

The ordinary and the everyday tend to be obscured by the veil of familiarity, what we know well can seem dull and boring. How can we experience the familiar as strange and exciting? The only way is through looking again and looking hard, perhaps seeing some things as if for the first time. In this way we may be able to communicate that freshness to others and so make them see 'for the first time' too.

The writers in this section of the book use their own powers of observation to stimulate our own. Think about how much history has been contained in one place or about the incredible stories that might be attached to a single object. They are helping us to appreciate what we usually take for granted.

Once we begin to observe the world with more intensity then nothing can be the same again. The things and places are not different, but we are, and, because we are, so we can bring to life what we have observed. This section is full of examples of the kind of writing that we might try for ourselves. It is demanding and challenging; it is rarely easy because it does not come naturally. For instance, how do you make a fridge interesting?

There is an old saying about beauty being in the eye of the beholder and the same is surely true for dullness. If you are determined to be bored or dull then no wonder that the world looks the same! If you work hard on observing, you may reveal new interests. It is worth looking closely here at how the writers refuse to let us see the familiar - they ask that we look again.

Some of the topics covered in this section are less obvious and familiar to us, and so the writer has to make them real. This can mean using the language of poetry to strike us with an intriguing image, or setting out and ordering a complex process so that we can comprehend and appreciate it. There are many ways to turn careful observation into good writing, and this section attempts to show some of them.

Anne Frank with a Telephone
John Pilger

- Work with someone else and look at the essay together. What do you think the writer wants us to feel once we have read about Nasreen and her family? Why do you think he chose this family to describe when he makes it clear that there are other families with the same kinds of experience from that area? Does reading the story make you want to do something? What could you do if you wanted to help Nasreen and her family? Why do you think he calls the essay *Anne Frank with a Telephone*.
- Look at this assignment only if you are interested in studying the article in detail. John Pilger describes a horrible situation in this piece and he clearly wants to make us feel its horror, but how does he do this? Work with a partner and examine the article very carefully as a piece of writing. First look closely at the opening. What is established in the first paragraph? Second, what is actually described in the whole piece and what do we learn from it? Third, how does Pilger use other peoples' voices in the story of the family to influence our reading? Once you have considered all these points, think about *how* this article works on us. It is not an argumentative essay, it is a description of a situation but it does contain an argument. Do you agree?
- When do you think this piece was written? Could it be written today?
- What happens next in the story? You might continue it from Nasreen's point of view in her diary and letters, or you could write as the author producing another piece about the family. Perhaps you feel that another kind of journalist would write about the family from quite a different point of view?
- Do you feel strongly about injustice? Are there injustices that you know about? Could you use your own experiences or perhaps your imagination to write a piece like John Pilger's? Such a story would need a considerable amount of work including some research before you could produce a final version; is there a subject you feel strongly enough about to write in this way?

Two Ways of Seeing a River
Mark Twain

This piece comes from *Life on the Mississippi* (1883), Twain's autobiographical account of his years spent as a riverboat captain on the Mississippi river. Mark Twain is one of the most famous American writers of the nineteenth century. He produced such comic classics as *Huckleberry Finn* and *The Adventures of Tom Sawyer*.

- Work in a small group and try to identify what is so different about the two descriptions of the river. Think about the language and mood of the first description and contrast them with those of the second one. What has changed in the writer's attitude to his subject? What do you think the final point about the doctor's view is meant to add to our response? Are both descriptions of the water equally good or do you prefer one to the other? Can they be judged on the same basis?
- Choose either of the two views of the river and continue the description for another paragraph. Before you do this make some notes for yourself on the way Twain describes the look of the river itself and especially the kinds of descriptive words that he chooses. You might find it useful to have the comments of some others from the class on your continuation before you write a final draft. If you feel your continuation is promising, you might extend it into a continuation of the journey itself.
- Can you develop your writing by thinking about this description of the river and considering your own work? Try out these ideas. Choose something, perhaps an object or a place, which you think is interesting and worth describing and then write two views of it, one which stresses its importance to you, and the other which is simply informative, e.g. an engine, a piece of music, a landscape, a building, a sport, a picture.

Song of the Light-bulb
Kamimura Hajime

Kamimura Hajime was born in 1910 near Nagasaki, Japan. For many years he has run a bookshop in northern Kyushu.

- Work with a partner on this poem and consider what difference it would have made to the poem if the word 'secretly' had been left out.
- What do you notice about the way the poet uses light and dark in the poem?
- Continue the poem and describe what happens when the man gets home.
- Imagine a situation in which an object plays an important, though minor part, and write your own 'Song of ...'.

The Fridge
Boris Slutsky

A Ukranian poet, Slutsky served in the Red Army during the Second World War. He is best known for the simplicity and directness of his writing.

- What kind of machine is the fridge, according to Slutsky? What does he compare it to?
- Choose a familiar machine that you know well and describe it in a way that will make your reader look at it again. Consider Slutsky's point about a future robot revolution; would your machine be loyal to humanity in a machine uprising?
- Perhaps the poet is wrong about fridges. Perhaps you see them as threatening or exciting? Write your own piece about the fridge in which you give it quite a different character.

Downpipes
Novella Matveyeva

Novella Matveyeva is a Russian poet, born near Leningrad, who has been writing poetry since childhood. She also composes and performs her own songs. She is unusual amongst Soviet poets for her emphasis on the fantastic.

● The poem seems at first to be just about the drainpipes of a house in the rain and, at one level, so it is. Read it through several times and observe what else is mentioned. Note the other images in the poem and then begin to piece together an idea of the other subjects you think the poem is concerned with.
● This is a very visual poem; imagine that you are going to make a short film to be shown as the words are spoken. Write a storyboard describing the images that you would show to accompany the words.
● Choose some feature of a house that strikes your imagination and write a piece about it and what it makes you think of.
● You might prefer to select another kind of physical detail that stimulates your thinking and provides you with a visual image as a starting point.

A Postcard from France
(editors' title)
Sylvia Plath

This postcard was written not for publication but simply as a message to the writer's mother. (For more information on the author see also the poem *Mirror* on page 103.)

● Work with a partner and compare the images you 'see' as you read the words of the postcard. Do you both 'see' the same scene, as described by Plath?
● What do you think the final French phrase means?
● Whilst you work on the next few suggestions, remember that Sylvia Plath managed to fit in over 300 words on her card!
● Think back to a memorable visit you have made and write a postcard now that you might have written at the time. Think about how you might imitate the way Plath crams in so much vivid detail.
● Write an imaginary postcard from a place you have never seen but would like to visit.
● Think of some postcards that might have been written by famous historical figures. You might be able to write some amusing cards! For example, Julius Caesar's impressions of Britain; Columbus' first card from the 'New' World, and so on.

The Driver Ants
Thomas Belt

Thomas Belt (1832-78) was an English geologist and gold-mining expert who travelled widely in Australia, Siberia, and the United States of America.

● Prepare a one-minute talk to give to a small group on the habits of the Driver Ants.
● These ants work together very effectively. Do you find their team work admirable or are you horrified by it? Do the ants remind you of people in any way?

● This piece of writing is precise in all its details. The writer must have observed the ants very closely. Can you think of any topic about which you have such precise and detailed knowledge? Try writing a description like this one after you have spent some time observing your chosen subject with care.

● In some ways scientists and poets are very similar - they both try for exact expression in their language. Write a poem based on Thomas Belt's description and then consider the two pieces together. How easily or usefully can they be compared?

Running
Linford Christie

Linford Christie is one of Britain's best-known athletes; a European champion and a UK record holder. He is a very experienced athlete who has competed all over the world. This is his contribution to a book about becoming a better athlete, where he tries to give us an insight into the techniques of sprint running.

● If you were going to run a sprint race would you now approach it in a different way because of what you have read?

● Read the extract again and make a ten-point list of key things to do for anyone interested in becoming a good sprinter.

● Write a description of a sprint race or a particular runner drawing on some of the insights that you have gained from this expert opinion.

● Think of an area of experience that you feel you know well. Try writing a piece which would help someone who is keen to learn about it but who needs a lot of advice. Look closely at the way Christie breaks down the process of running into small, separate sections. This may be helpful to you in trying to complete your description.

Witnessing

This section is devoted to those writers who have witnessed, in reality or in imagination, something that they felt they had to write about. We have all had experiences that we can vividly recall, not always easily because sometimes the memory may be disturbing, even tragic. Writing about such experiences can be a very important way of dealing with them but a great deal of careful work may need to be done in order to communicate what the experience actually means. The examples in this section show how some writers have tried to describe and deal with experiences of this nature.

Not all these shared experiences are disturbing or tragic; they can be strange or simply funny. You could undoubtedly produce many odd and amusing descriptions about the way you grew up or the things your family and friends got up to.

Another important consideration is imagination. You do not need to have experienced something yourself to have a true sense of what it was like. You can draw on everything that you know about that experience and by using the power of your imagination you can become a 'witness' to what happened. Writing down what you experience in your imagination can be as much of a challenge as trying to describe some vivid, 'real' event. You may need to draft your ideas and discuss them with others in order to make the most of your imaginative vision.

Whether writing about a real or imagined event no description is merely a record. When you have witnessed or imagined a scene that you want to communicate to others you may also have an opinion, a point of view or a careful argument to put across as part of your writing. The reason for describing a hanging or a war is often more about persuading readers to change their views than to record what happened.

Every writer is a witness and every witness can learn to write successfully about what happened.

A Hanging
George Orwell

George Orwell lived from 1903 to 1950. Orwell had a varied and dramatic life, writing on a tremendous range of topics in numerous styles. He produced many essays but is best known for his novels *Nineteen Eighty Four* and *Animal Farm*. This piece was written as a result of his time as a policeman in Burma when it was ruled by the British.

● Before you read this extract have a piece of paper in front of you to jot down your reactions. The following points may be helpful:
  - What does the title make you think about? Are you in favour of capital punishment?
  - What impression do you form of the prisoner in the first five paragraphs?
  - How do you feel about the interruption caused by the dog?
  - Do you agree with the ideas written about in paragraph ten?
  - Do you find the joke funny in paragraph twenty-two?
● How do you feel after your first reading? Is your answer to the first question any different now?
● Look over the story again and re-read your notes. How clear are your first impressions? Do they need revising after a second reading?
● Work with someone else to consider the essay in some depth. What point do you think Orwell is trying to make? Can you find clear evidence of his point of view in the essay? The title is simply *A Hanging* - would you have given it this title? Finally, can you put this piece into a category e.g. is it a story, a description, does it have an argument? Is it all these things?
● In *A Hanging* Orwell seems to be putting forward his views on capital punishment through what at first appears to be a story of an execution. Could you express your own strong feelings about a subject through a

story? In other words, could you persuade your readers to agree with you through the message of the story you write?
● Imagine you are a journalist who is covering this story. You could interview the people who witnessed the execution (including Orwell himself) and use their views and comments in your story. Think about where such an article might appear and consider the audience you would be aiming at.

The Arrest of Dr Crippen
Captain H. G. Kendall

Captain Kendall was the master of the Canadian Pacific liner *Montrose*, on which Crippen was arrested in 1910.

● Improvise the next few lines of the story in which Kendall explains how he realised that Robinson was really Crippen.
● Write and record the radio news broadcast of that day which describes the arrest of Crippen.
● Work with a partner and role play Crippen and a radio interviewer asking him about his capture and about how he feels now.
● Work in a group and decide together how to make this description into an exciting opening to a film about Crippen's life. The director has asked you, the writing team, to begin at this point so that the audience will always know that Crippen will be caught. When the film opens the audience will not know exactly what is going on. Can you make the scene intriguing by not giving away too much information but by building up suspense?

Not My Best Side
U. A. Fanthorpe

St George and the Dragon
Paolo Uccello

U. A. Fanthorpe is an English poet, born in 1929. She published her first collection in 1978. Fanthorpe has become highly acclaimed for her ingenious and thought-provoking style. Paolo Uccello was an Italian artist who lived from 1396 -1475. He worked in a variety of ways and is best remembered for his oil paintings of scenes like this one and of battle pictures. His pictures can be found in galleries around the world.

● Have a close look at the picture before you read the poem. Work in a small group and see if you can agree on the details and subject of the picture. These questions might help to guide discussion:
  - Would you know the subject of the poem even without the title?
  - What is the artist trying to show us about each of the figures through the way they are represented? (Think about size, movement, position, expression and so on.)
  - What do you notice about the way the figures are reacting to each other?
  - How did the situation arise? What is going to happen next?
● Work in a group of at least three and prepare a reading of the poem. This will provide you with a different voice for each character. Decide together on how each character is feeling and their views of the other two. How can these elements be expressed in your reading? Look at the picture. Does it provide you with any clues?

- It might be suggested that the picture represents male courage and strength rescuing female frailty and weakness. Does the class, or the group you are working with, agree with this statement? Has the poet changed your view of the picture at all or has she simply written a new version of the story? Do you think Uccello would have approved of Fanthorpe's poem?
- Write your own version of the picture/poem by creating three new verses by each character. Alternatively, find a reproduction of another painting and try writing a similar piece using the characters from that picture as a basis.
- Both the poem and the picture are versions of a famous episode from history/legend. Write a version of your own, perhaps written from an unusual and challenging viewpoint. Your piece could be serious or comic, or in any style you like.

The Cry
Amano Tadashi

A Japanese poet, born in 1909, Amano Tadashi has been Director of the Library at Nara Womens' College for many years.

- Do you think that this is really a moral story? What do you feel the poet is writing about, through the example of the tiniest insect? Is your reaction that the insect deserved its fate, or do you sympathise with it?
- In a way the poem is about fear. What are your own particular fears? Could you write about one of them honestly?
- The poet imagines a situation where he is the witness and so we are there too through his poem. Try writing a poem or descriptive piece which witnesses some strange and revealing incident. Let your imagination wander through possibilities before deciding on your subject.

A Life in Pictures
Don McCullin

The photograph and accompanying comments have been produced by someone who has devoted his life to recording some of the horrors of the modern world. They deserve a close look.

- Spend some time on your own noting down what you actually see in the picture, then compare your ideas with a partner.
- Move on to the writing as well and discuss it with your partner. What impression do you build up of Don McCullin? What makes him take such grim pictures?
- Imagine that you are at the scene but that you have to report it in words - you have no camera. You are either a print or a radio journalist and so you will write a description or speak or tape one.
- The photograph is a powerful image that might be used in a variety of ways. Can you keep its 'truth' but suggest how its power might be used? For example in a propaganda picture, or an advertising campaign for charity.
- Let your imagination work on the idea of powerful images, perhaps

discussing your ideas with others. Can you select some images that you already know and then write some accompanying text to go with the pictures in their new context. Here are some suggestions: a history textbook; a film poster; the cover of a novel; a record sleeve; a military recruitment poster; a leaflet for a charity; a personal photo album.

Living Jim Crow
(editor's title)
Richard Wright

Richard Wright was born in Mississippi and wrote novels portraying the experience of the black American in the ghetto. His novels are powerful and explicit in their use of both emotional and political argument.

● Work in a small group and discuss the extract together. Judging from the experiences that Wright describes, do you think that his family was right to advise him to 'stay in your place'?
● Imagine that a child, perhaps 10 years old, had just read this piece and asked you to explain it. What could you say to help a young child understand the attitudes shown by the white people?
● Some people might suggest that this piece of writing is an example from the past and simply stirs up bad feelings. Do you think that it is a good idea to read about experiences like these in school or not? If someone wanted to ban this item would you support the idea?
● Richard Wright describes his experiences very vividly. He remembers what happened so clearly because it was so unjust. Can you recall examples of injustice from your own life (the injustice need not have been directed at you)? Write about your memories or produce a story about the injustice suffered by someone in childhood.

The Amateur Scientist
Richard Feynman

Richard Feynman is one of those remarkable people who combine many talents. As well as being a world famous scientist he is also a very entertaining writer. This extract shows both his scientific knowledge and his ability as a comic writer.

● Work in a small group and examine this extract together. How is it written? Is it scientific writing or a piece of entertainment?
● Take any paragraph and rewrite it in what you would consider a scientific style. Compare your paragraph with someone else's (preferably the same paragraph). What differences have you each made in order to 'take out' the humour?
● Would this kind of writing be appropriate for one of your science text books?
● Imagine Richard Feynman gives a radio talk about science. Write an extract from his talk using *The Amateur Scientist* as your model.
● Have you dabbled in science in any way outside the classroom? Have you ever had amusing moments in science classes at school? Try to write a piece that conveys something interesting about science but also makes entertaining writing.

Making

We have all had the frustrating experience of not being able to understand how to do something: perhaps we are baffled by a set of instructions for a new gadget, or cannot comprehend the manual which explains how to operate a machine. Writing clearly about how things should happen is vital for all of us and it is a skill which should not be underestimated.

The problem may be that the writer knows so much about the subject that he or she cannot remember what it was like to be ignorant about the topic. In this way being an expert can make someone a bad writer. Being a good explainer in writing is like being a good teacher. It does not matter how much teachers know if they cannot make their classes understand new ideas.

Thinking about your audience is always important for a writer but in this case you need a special kind of sensitivity and care. Will the audience understand the special words you are using? Would these ideas be better communicated by a diagram or a flowchart? Can you break the description down into several clear steps which anyone can follow? It is also important to consider the difficulty of writing about ideas and attitudes. How do you explain to someone what it feels like to be a teenager in a world dominated by adults?

Much of the writing in this section is especially helpful for thinking through the kinds of writing that you may have to do when you are at work. Once you become knowledgeable in your job, whatever it is, you may need to write down information for others. This information will need to be absolutely accurate if the reader is to carry out the action which is necessary. Think about how vital some written information about operating a machine might be or how precise the explanation of customer requirements should be to understand the importance of accuracy.

The writing of this section covers a wide range of approaches but it is all about how we make things or how we make things happen, from the technical precision of the telephone to the verbal artistry of a poem.

Making Your Own Chocolate
Sandra Boynton

Electrics
Harry Greene

These extracts come from information books which use words and illustrations to describe their subjects. The first is a light-hearted look at making chocolate; the second tries to provide information to help us to understand and deal with the systems we depend on every day.

● Spend some time reading and studying these descriptions. They are factually accurate, but how easy are they to understand? How important are the pictures in each case? Are the pieces illustrated in the same way?

● It is always difficult to explain a complicated process in simple language, even with pictures to help. Discuss with a partner whether you find it easy to follow instructions about putting together something you have bought. What is difficult about explaining a process to someone else through writing?

● Work on your own or with others for this assignment. Select a process that people need to understand, e.g. anything from wiring a plug to ironing a shirt, and design a leaflet to explain the process. You can make your leaflet straightforward and serious or you can try to give it a humorous style; either way you can use illustrations to help your description.

● You might prefer to undertake a 'real' task. Ask around at school about the problems teachers have with certain explanations e.g. safety in the laboratory, fire drills, using a word processor, finding a particular book in the library. Design a leaflet to make one of these tasks easier.

How to Kill a Bull at a Fiesta
Matthew Kay

This essay comes from an American book for college students. The book provides examples of writing to discuss and consider (rather like this book). We chose it because it deals with a very gory, dramatic subject in a matter of fact way. Writing like this provides you with a very clear description, but what does it leave out?

● Is this a good description of a bull fight (it does not matter whether you have been to such a fight or not)? Do you think that the matter of fact description makes for a good piece of writing? Would you have preferred more emotion or comment from the writer?

● Write about the same scene in a variety of ways. You could either write all the views yourself or you might work in a group and each take one aspect. Here are some possibilities: a spectator who enjoys the spectacle; a spectator who is horrified by the cruelty; the matador; the picador; a banderillo; the bull itself.

● There are still many blood sports in the world; for example, Britain is well known for fox-hunting. Do you have strong feelings on this subject? If you do, try describing a typical scene from such a sport in a direct way, in order to persuade your reader of its cruelty.

A Man Who Writes a Poem
Tamura Ryûichi

A Japanese poet born in Tokyo in 1923, Tamura Ryûichi has been a full time writer for many years and has spent some time in America teaching the art of writing poetry. He is one of Japan's best known poets.

● What do you think the poet is trying to explain about poetry writing through his description of the process of writing?
● Can you draw a picture which represents this poem?
● How do you write poems?
● Imagine that suddenly everyone in the country had to read a poem and write one of their own every day. What would happen, and what difference would it make to life?

Young, Gifted and Black
Beverley Naidoo

Beverley Naidoo is a writer from South Africa who has worked in Britain for a number of years, writing journalism and fiction. She has also edited collections for schools. This essay comes from such a collection and is a personal account of her own involvement with teaching.

● We have included this essay in the section called 'Making' because we feel that the writer is describing her attempt to build something for the children she worked with. Do you think this is the right place for it, or should it be in a different section?
● Try writing about the school from a different point of view. How would the children see their school? What about the views of the other teachers? Perhaps you might write as a visitor having a look around the school.
● This essay is also about racism. Write a letter to the author, expressing your opinions on the topic after reading her comments.

We are not a Sub-Species ...
Lois McNay

This feature appeared in *The Guardian* newspaper several years ago.

● Work in a small group and decide how far you agree with the points made by the writer. Have things improved for teenagers since the feature was published?
● Try writing a definition of a teenager or of the different sorts of teenager that you feel you can identify. You need not try to write seriously if you would rather make fun of the whole idea of 'the teenager'.
● How do you feel young people are portrayed in the media? Produce a typical newspaper article involving someone in their late teens.

Michael Jackson
(editors' title)
Kobena Mercer

Kobena Mercer teaches at the Centre for Caribbean Studies in London. This is an extract from a long article that describes and analyses the production of the famous *Thriller* video. We chose it because it provides an interesting example of how to write about the way in which an image of a person is created.

● This is not an easy passage; it uses some difficult words. After you have read it work with a partner and identify words that you feel need some explanation. Compare your needs with another pair, or use a dictionary to help you. Once you have worked on the passage try to suggest simpler words to substitute for those you found difficult.
● What in your opinion has happened to Michael Jackson as he has become more famous?
● Work in a group and discuss whether you think that Jackson is really unusual or whether he is in fact typical of what happens to young people who become rich and famous. Do you think that the public has a right to know about the lives of people like Jackson; is this the price of fame?

● Choose someone very famous (you do not need to like this person). Find out what you can about them and then write a piece providing as much information as you can but also try to explain his or her extraordinary success.

Changing

The only truly constant part of life is change. As we write and as you read we are all changing. Yet writing about ideas and feelings seems to fix them forever so that we can at least examine them closely whenever we wish to. Even then, however, each reading may be different.

Because it is always present, change is always fascinating. Writers have tried to capture it in endless ways and to resist it by producing a 'final version' of a poem or a book. Even one of those irritating comments about you that you have probably heard so often - "Haven't you grown!" or "She looks more like her mother every day!" - are examples of that fascination with change. People tend to notice change when it is at its most obvious, so that is why a photograph album that has pictures of an older generation makes everyone laugh at the hairstyles, the clothes, even the expressions on faces.

In some ways we are more aware of change than at any previous stage of human history. We look back for only a few years and we see how transport or technology have developed. The same may be true of our understanding of writing. Only 150 years ago a tiny proportion of the world could read and write; now every country recognises the importance of these fundamental skills. Every adult needs to understand not only how to write but also how writing works.

The writing in this section helps us to think about change and also about recording it. Some pieces describe how the world is being transformed, others reveal changes through comparison and contrast. Some extracts simply record experience and we are left to judge what has happened since then and what may yet happen to us. Your own writing may become a record of change for you. As the photograph album shows physical changes, so writing reveals changes of attitude and increasing maturity.

If you look through the whole of this book you will find an incredible range of writing. In certain ways it all helps us to understand change. Every description is an attempt to capture, to freeze, to fix, to explain. However good the writing, it can only partly succeed, and this is a very helpful message to us; even the best writers might do it differently another time. If we make a real effort now, perhaps producing several versions of a piece of writing before being satisfied, then we will have learned something in the process.

Orang-utan
Judith Nicholls

Judith Nicholls writes for children and for adults. She regularly runs workshops in schools, working closely with pupils and students of all ages. This piece comes from *The Guardian* newspaper's educational supplement. You will notice that Nicholl's comments about the drafts of the poem are written mainly to help teachers think about pupils' poetry.

● Work in a group and look at the various drafts of the poem *without reading the poet's comments*. What do you feel has changed between the various drafts of the poem? Are all the changes improvements?
● Continue working in your group and study Judith Nicholls' comments on her different drafts. Try to sum up in one sentence what she reveals about drafting.
● Find a picture of an orang-utan and discuss with a partner whether you feel the poem is accurate as a description of this particular animal.
● Try an experiment with your own writing. Choose a topic for a poem, perhaps a description of a creature, a place or a machine might be suitable, and then have several goes at 'getting it right'. Produce your drafts on different pieces of paper and when you feel that you have reached the final stage have a look at them all. You could then write a commentary showing how your ideas have gradually changed or you could do this by explaining your changes to a partner. Is the way you work similar to the way Judith Nicholls works?

If I Were a Man
Charlotte Perkins Gilman

Charlotte Perkins Gilman was a novelist, short story writer, editor and journalist who was writing in America at the turn of the century. She is best known for her study, *Women and Economics* which analyses the social, political, and economic situation for women. This story was first published in 1914.

● As you can see this story was written at the beginning of this century. Spend some time on the story, examining what it is saying and also how it is saying it. Work in a small group and check that you agree on the kind of experience that Mollie has when she changes into Gerald. What is actually different about life for her once she sees it through the eyes of a man? Would you all call this a 'feminist' story?
● Work with a partner and imagine that Mollie has changed back into herself. Improvise her conversation with Gerald when she describes her impressions of life as a man.
● Try writing the day from Gerald's point of view. Imagine that he has spent the day in Mollie's body; what were his experiences?
● Imagine that this situation happened to a modern day woman or man. Tell one of their stories of a day in the body of the other sex.
● How much has changed since 1914? Discuss with others whether you feel we now live in a society where there is real equality of opportunity. A good question to begin with might be 'Who is best suited to bringing up small children?'
● Work with a partner of the opposite sex. You both have to write a

description of a typical day in the life of the other. Read each other's description and discuss the results.

The Silent Three of St Botolphs
Posy Simmons

● Working together decide what you think of the cartoon. Do you find it simply amusing or is it really making a serious and important point? Does it exaggerate the truth or is it showing an article that could still be written?
● Imagine that Wendy Weber and her husband George write a letter to the local paper pointing out all that was wrong with the newspaper report. Write the letter and an accompanying comment from the paper's editor.
● Working with others consider how this story might be continued in some way in next week's cartoon strip. Try deciding on some of the images and writing the voice balloons to go with them.
● Working with others bring in some examples of your local paper and look at some of the stories. Can you find any examples where men and women are described in a 'trivialising way'?

Woman
Fu Hsüan

We're Only Women
Novella Matveyeva

Fu Hsüan was a Chinese poet who lived about 1500 years ago. Novella Matveyeva is a Russian poet.

● What do these poems have in common?
● The poems were written more than 1500 years apart and in very different cultures. Does this suggest anything to you about their common theme?
● Imagine that there is to be an advertising campaign to make people think about the relationships of men and women in more depth. Your job is to choose one of these poems to be used as a poster poem on trains. Which would you choose and why? How would you advise on the design of the poster?
● Try writing your own poem and making it into a poster.

**Wilfred Owen
1893-1918**
Jon Stallworthy

Jon Stallworthy is a writer and editor who has a special interest in the 1914 -1918 Great War.

● What have you learned about Owen's attitude to the Great War from this brief biography? Do you think he wanted to be a fighter?
● Owen once wrote that his poetry was 'not about heroes'. Do you look on Owen himself as a hero?
● This piece is a very short biography of a famous writer. How do you think a biographer collects information in order to write a biography? Work in a small group and consider how to trace someone's life. Another important point is interest. You may not be especially inspired by a poet who died in the Great War but there may be other individuals who attract you - could you write a biography? What would make it interesting?

- Choose someone who intrigues you (he or she need not be famous) and write a biography. You could look in encyclopedias for examples of short biographies.

Voices and Images of the Great War
ed. *Lyn MacDonald*

These extracts were all written by 'ordinary' people in an extraordinary situation. They are attempts to describe the events and the scenes that faced soldiers and civilians in the Great War.

- Imagine that you were 'at the front'. Write a letter home to your family about the life you are leading.
- Choose any one of the extracts and use your imagination to continue the writing.
- Work in a group for this assignment. Imagine that it is the year 2013. Next year will be the hundredth anniversary of the beginning of the Great War. Your group is to make a documentary (for radio or television, you decide which) to let people know what happened. What kind of programme would you make and how would you use these extracts in the programme?
- Work as a group to prepare readings of these extracts for the rest of the class to hear. You may want to add some commentary of your own to link the passages.

LIST OF TEXTS BY THEME

Accidents
Ian McEwan   'A Near Miss'

Adolescence
Lois McNay   'We are not a Sub-Species ...'
Alice Walker   'My Daughter Smokes'
Richard Wright   'Living Jim Crow'

Animals
Matthew Kay   'How to Kill a Bull at a Fiesta'
Judith Nicholls   'Orang-utan'

Autobiography
Malcolm X   'Autobiography'
Angela Carter   'Tokyo Pastoral'

Biography
Kobena Mercer   'Michael Jackson'
Jon Stallworthy   'Wilfred Owen'
John Aubrey   'Sir Thomas More'

Change
Charlotte Perkins Gilman   'If I Were a Man'

Children
Richard Wright   'Living Jim Crow'

Crime
George Orwell   'A Hanging'
Captain H. G. Kendall   'The Arrest of Dr Crippen'

Family
Elizabeth Jennings   'Resemblances'
John Pilger   'Anne Frank with a Telephone'
Alice Walker   'My Daughter Smokes'
Richard Wright   'Living Jim Crow'
John Aubrey   'Sir Thomas More'

Fashion
U. A. Fanthorpe   'Not My Best Side'
Kobena Mercer   'Michael Jackson'

Food
Sandra Boynton   'Making Your Own Chocolate'

Humour
Wendy Cope   'The Lavatory Attendant'
Richard Feynman   'The Amateur Scientist'
Craig Raine   'The Butcher'
Angela Carter   'Tokyo Pastoral'
John Aubrey   'Sir Thomas More'

Individual
Takano Kikuo   'I'm'
Sylvia Plath   'Mirror'
Malcolm X   'Autobiography'

Loneliness
Hajime Kamimura   'Song of the Light-Bulb'
Amano Tadashi   'The Cry'

Love
Hajime Kamimura   'Song of the Light-Bulb'

Men
Charlotte Perkins Gilman   'If I Were a Man'
Malcolm X   'Autobiography'

Music
Kobena Mercer   'Michael Jackson'

Nature
Thomas Belt   'The Driver Ants'
Richard Feynman   'The Amateur Scientist'
Mark Twain   'Two Ways of Seeing a River'
Judith Nicholls   'Orang-utan'

Photography
Don McCullin   'A Life in Pictures'

Poetry
Tamura Ryûichi   'A Man Who Writes a Poem'
Judith Nicholls   'Orang-utan'

Punishment
George Orwell 'A Hanging'
Captain H. G. Kendall 'The Arrest of Dr Crippen'

Race
Langston Hughes 'Theme for English B'
Kobena Mercer 'Michael Jackson'
Beverley Naidoo 'Young, Gifted and Black'
George Orwell 'A Hanging'
John Pilger 'Anne Frank with a Telephone'
Richard Wright 'Living Jim Crow'
Malcolm X 'Autobiography'
Angela Carter 'Tokyo Pastoral'
Ntozake Shange 'my father is a retired magician'

School
Langston Hughes 'Theme for English B'
Beverley Naidoo 'Young, Gifted and Black'

Science
Richard Feynman 'The Amateur Scientist'
Harry Greene 'Electrics'

Smoking
Alice Walker 'My Daughter Smokes'

Sport
Matthew Kay 'How to Kill a Bull at a Fiesta'
Linford Christie 'Running'

Technology
Sandra Boynton 'Making Your Own Chocolate'
Boris Slutsky 'The Fridge'
Harry Greene 'Electrics'

Teenagers
Lois McNay 'We are not a Sub-Species ...'

Time
Ian McEwan 'A Near Miss'

Travel
Ian McEwan 'A Near Miss'
Don McCullin 'A Life in Pictures'
Sylvia Plath 'A Postcard from France'
Mark Twain 'Two Ways of Seeing a River'
Angela Carter 'Tokyo Pastoral'

War
Lyn MacDonald 'Voices and Images of the
   Great War'
Don McCullin 'A Life in Pictures'
Jon Stallworthy 'Wilfred Owen'

Weather
Novella Matveyeva 'Downpipes'

Women
U. A. Fanthorpe 'Not My Best Side'
Charlotte Perkins Gilman 'If I Were a Man'
Fu Hsüan 'Woman'
Novella Matveyeva 'We're Only Women'

Work
Craig Raine 'The Butcher'

Writing
Tamura Ryûichi 'A Man Who Writes a Poem'
Judith Nicholls 'Orang-utan'

INDEX OF AUTHORS
AND ILLUSTRATORS

ACKNOWLEDGEMENTS

The editors and publishers wish to thank the following who have kindly granted permission for the use of copyright material:-

BBC Enterprises for an extract from *On the House* by Harry Greene published by BBC Books.

Faber & Faber Ltd. for the poem 'Mirror' by Sylvia Plath from *Collected Poems 1956-1963*, edited by Ted Hughes (1981); for the poem 'The Lavatory Attendant' by Wendy Cope from *Making Cocoa for Kingley Amis* (1986); and for the extract 'A Postcard from France' by Sylvia Plath from *Letters Home*, edited by Aurelia Plath (1978).

Elaine Feinstein for the translation of the poem 'The Fridge' by Boris Slutsky from *Post-War Russian Poetry*, edited by Daniel Weissbort.

HarperCollins Publishers Ltd. for the poem 'Woman' by Fu Hsüan, edited and translated by Arthur Waley and published by Allen & Unwin (1969); for the essay 'Young, Gifted and Black' by Beverley Naidoo from *Free As I Know*, published by Bell & Hyman (1987), and with W. W. Norton & Co. Inc. for the extract 'The Amateur Scientist' from *Surely You're Joking, Mr Feynman! Adventures of a Curious Character*, edited by Edward Hutchings (1985).

A.M. Heath & Co. Ltd. on behalf of the Estate of the late Sonia Brownell Orwell and Martin Secker & Warburg Ltd. for the extract 'A Hanging' from *The Collected Works of George Orwell*.

David Higham Associates Ltd. on behalf of Langston Hughes for the poem 'Theme for English B' from *Black Voices: Poetry - An Anthology of Afro-American Literature* published by Mentor Books (1968); on behalf of Elizabeth Jennings for the poem 'Resemblances' from *A Sense of the World* published by Andre Deutsch Ltd. (1958), and on behalf of Alice Walker for 'My Daughter Smokes' from *Living By The Word: Selected Writings 1973-1987* (1988) published by The Women's Press Ltd.

Lois McNay for the article 'We are not a Sub-Species' published in *The Guardian* 1978.

Methuen London for the poem 'my father is a retired magician' by Ntozake Shange from *Nappy Edges* (1978).

Judith Nicholls for the article 'Orang-utan' published in *The Guardian*, 8 January, 1991.

Oxford University Press for the poem 'The Butcher' by Craig Raine from *The Onion, Memory* (1978), and for the extract from a letter by Wilfred Owen from *Wilfred Owen: Selected Letters* edited by John Bell and Harold Owen (1985).

Penguin Books Ltd. for poems from *Post-War Japanese Poetry* edited and translated by Harry and Lynn Guest and Kajima Shozo. Copyright © Harry Guest, Lynn Guest and Kajima Shozo, 1972, 'I'm' by Takano Kikuo, 'Song of the Lightbulb' by Kamimura Hajime, 'The Cry' by Amano Tadashi, and 'A Man Who Writes a Poem' by Tamura Ryûichi.

Peters Fraser & Dunlop Ltd. on behalf of Posy Simmonds for the cartoon 'The Silent Three of St Botolph's' from *Mrs Weber's Diary* published by Jonathan Cape Ltd.

Laurence Pollinger Ltd. on behalf of Lynn Macdonald for extracts from *Voices and Images of The Great War 1914-1918* published by Michael Joseph Ltd. (1988).

Random Century Group on behalf of the Estate of Wilfred Owen for an extract from the poem 'The Send Off' from *Anthem for Doomed Youth* by Wilfred Owen, published by Chatto & Windus Ltd.; for the extract 'A Near Miss' from *The Child in Time* by Ian McEwan, published by Jonathan Cape Ltd.

Martin Secker & Warburg Ltd. for the extract 'Sir Thomas More' by John Aubrey from *Aubrey's Brief Lives* edited by Oliver Lawson Dick (1949).

Jon Stallworthy for the extract 'Wilfred Owen, 1893-1918' from *The Lost Voices of World War 1* edited by Tim Cross, published by Bloomsbury Publishing Ltd. (1989).

Abner Stein on behalf of Don McCullin for the extract and photograph from *A Life in Pictures*.

Virago Press Ltd. for the extract 'Tokyo Pastoral' by Angela Carter.

Every effort has been made to trace all the copyright holders but if any have been inadvertently overlooked the publishers will be pleased to make the neccessary arrangement at the first opportunity.

Photographic Acknowledgements

The editors and publishers wish to acknowledge, with thanks, the following photographic sources:

Mansell Collection p8; Popperfoto p41, p98; Topham Picture Library p14; UPI/Bettman Newsphotos p59.